COACHING LEGACY OF CHAMPIONS

CHRIS RIDLEY

COACHING LEGACY OF CHAMPIONS

Copyright © 2024 by Chris Ridley

All rights reserved. No part of this publication may be reproduced, distributed, or transmitted in any form or by any means, including photocopying, recording, or other electronic or mechanical methods, without the prior written permission of the copyright holder, except in the case of brief quotations embodied in critical reviews and certain other noncommercial uses permitted by copyright law. For permission requests, write to the publisher, addressed "Attention: Permissions Coordinator," at the address below.

Softcover - 978-1-64318-134-9

1097 N 400 Rd
Baldwin City, KS, 66006
www.imperiumpublishing.com

COACHING LEGACY OF CHAMPIONS

CHRIS RIDLEY

INTRODUCTION

What's your next book going to be? You've written two books about Kansas high school football coaches. Are you staying in that zone? It's comfortable. You know what you're doing there. Folks seem to like the biographical stuff. These were the questions of others, and also questions I pondered myself.

I have relied on a local journalist's advice about writing—at least in relation to subject matter for books. Particularly biographies. A sports writer and journalist, my friend Rick Peterson provided me with great advice about my previous two books. He helped me immensely with tips about my first book. It was my first attempt, and I welcomed his suggestions. He gave me many wonderfully helpful suggestions about "Venable—Part Legend, All-American." More importantly, he assured me he thought I had substance and that folks would find the book interesting. It wasn't just a book about football. It definitely had a human interest side. As Pete and I were discussing my second book—"Never Seen a Finer Day" that chronologically captures the twenty-three football seasons Ron Bowen coached while at Washburn Rural High School and contains a bit about his prior teaching and initial coaching stints in Kansas—I wanted to tell a bit about the life of Bowen. Peterson gave me advice regarding that book as well. I feel like Bowen's book focused a lot on the impact he had on his students and the student-athletes he mentored all across the state of Kansas. While discussing that book, Rick kindly threw me his idea about a third story.

Peterson said, "You ought to write your next book about Kevin Hedberg."

That intrigued me.

It's fact that, for forty plus years (1980-2021), Hedberg undoubtedly had the biggest impact on the entire Topeka, Kansas tennis community. No kidding and no exaggeration. He was an excellent youth and high school tennis player, competing at Topeka High School during the late 1960s. He returned to Topeka as a tennis instructor, coaching numerous future high school tennis competitors. He was a division one collegiate tennis player on scholarship at the University of South Florida located in Tampa. He spent time working as a tennis professional for Topeka Country Club, a year as an assistant tennis pro in Houston, Texas, and a year as the Tennis Director/ Manager for the Kansas City Racquet Club. He then shifted his career gears and decided that he wanted to become a teacher. Not only a teacher of tennis—which continues today—but a high school coach and a classroom teacher as well. He's always been a person who taught tennis lessons to individuals and provided lessons for larger groups with his summer camps. It's just as important to mention the fact that Hedberg was also one of the most remarkable classroom teachers that I've ever had the honor of working alongside. Many colleagues and students share the same view. I'll let them be the storytellers later. Firsthand experience is always the best.

In 1991, I had the opportunity, as the athletic director at Topeka-Washburn Rural High School, to hire Kevin as a social studies teacher and tennis coach. He had already established himself as a very well-respected and good high school coach at Topeka-Seaman High School for the previous eleven years. His reputation in Topeka, Kansas, across Shawnee County and the whole state was that of a great teacher of fundamentals associated with tennis. When he wasn't coaching high school tennis in the fall and the spring, he was giving tennis lessons to most of Topeka's most accomplished tennis players. He was exceptionally gifted, working with anyone's level of tennis expertise and skills. His beginner-level programs have helped so many kids on a path toward playing competitive tennis or, for just as many, his teaching has allowed them to play for their own personal enjoyment. He's an ambassador for the sport that he loves and the sport that has given him so much for so many years. If you need to know the pulse of tennis in Kansas, past or present, Hedberg is your man. He feels strongly about Kansas's longstanding excellence in youth tennis and confidently says Kansas is recognized nationally as well for its young players' tennis abilities.

So, when we had an opening in social studies and we also needed a tennis coach, we interviewed ONE person for the position. Kevin Hedberg. After interim Principal Bill Edwards and I interviewed Kevin, we both looked at each other and said, "Why would we interview or hire anyone else?" We called our associate superintendent at the time, Mr. Dennis Shoemaker, and asked if it was necessary for us to interview anyone else. After we filled Shoemaker in on Hedberg's qualifications, experiences and recommendations—both as a tennis coach and in the classroom—he told us we could hire him. Bill Edwards was only a year older than Hedberg, and they both had graduated from the same high school, Topeka High. Edwards was filling the role of principal because our principal at the time, Bruce Thezan, was deployed in Desert Storm.

Hiring Hedberg was a major step for our high school tennis program that had already been one of dominance in Topeka and statewide. Bob Gladfelter had long overseen the development of the tennis teams. Bob—now an administrator himself—was elated to add Kevin to our staff. After Gladfelter coached one more girls season, he completely turned over the reins of the tennis program to Hedberg. Hedberg would coach the girls in the fall and boys in the spring. Bob knew a thing or two about coaching high school tennis. He himself is a member of the Kansas Tennis Hall of Fame. He knew what impact Hedberg could have in continuing the program's successful traditions, and he was correct. All our intuition appeared to be spot on. Bill Edwards always seemed to have a knack for knowing what candidate would best fit our needs. He could recognize good teachers through interviews. This one was an easy call for both of us.

Skip to 2021, and my major hurdle—which I fully expected—was Hedberg's reluctance to have a book written about him. As I would have predicted when we first spoke, Kevin's humility shone through. He never takes credit for his tennis teams' successes. And, granted, he has had a wealth of talent to pick from the majority of the years he's coached at Rural, but he has to make decisions about singles and doubles entries, and he has to utilize the standard coaching psychology and provide emotional support to his student-athletes. But coaching high school tennis requires more than just knowing the game. You are dealing with high school players. Some with egos. There are the expectations of some parents who aren't as objective as they should be. And high school tennis in Kansas—albeit an individual sport—has a team component built in with its team scoring design. Hedberg has masterfully helped kids understand the team component and is more than able to get them to realize and take pride in the fact that they have value and a role on the team that will help their teammates be successful. For all the team accomplishments, Hedberg is adept at recognizing each player's contributions.

As is the case in any sport, kids have to be willing to be placed in some roles they may not first embrace. Some will always be a bit reluctant to accept the roles they are given. But the majority of student-athletes Hedberg dealt with were unselfish and willing to sacrifice for the betterment of their team. This is not always the easiest sell in any sport. Unrelated to the team sacrifices, there are some rare occasions when kids have opted NOT to compete during the high school season. These rare few bypass competing at Regionals or State due to the timing conflict with the national junior tennis tournaments they want to enter. And some high-profile players feel they need this national exposure for possible scholarship and school selection. Hedberg has handled those rare instances as well as can be expected. And he supported what was in the best interest of the individual in those cases even if it could possibly affect team success at the state level. Sound like a juggling act? It was.

One thing I learned from writing about Coach Bowen was how elated he was over having so many of his former players recognized in a book—especially a book with historical implications. What high school athlete, now an adult, would not welcome some attention be given to their high school accomplishments. This was one selling point I gave to Coach Kevin Hedberg about how important this book would be. The importance of his kids' stories being told and having them recorded for posterity. That's important to coaches who coach for the sake of their kids and not for the sake of their own coaching ego. Hedberg is that kind of individual. Selfless.

Kevin and I met after school one November afternoon in 2021 for an adult beverage and a chat about the prospects of the book. Basically, I wanted to talk to Kevin about all the positives associated with having a book written that featured not only *his* life, but also the lives of the myriad of talented tennis players who played for him. Additionally, I saw it as an opportunity to capture bits and pieces about the many relationships his tennis and teaching has provided him. He's revered, probably more as a person, but also admired for being a tennis enthusiast.

It would be difficult to find a teaching colleague who would say anything disparaging about him. Equally difficult, it would be tough to find a student who has had a bad experience taking one of Hedberg's social studies classes. That's book-worthy in and of itself.

I fully expected that I might have had to put on my best salesman's hat to convince Hedberg to go along with this project, this story. Hedberg had already said he wouldn't tell me no. When we met, he handed me papers that contained all the tennis team and individual player accomplishments, including the time before he coached at Washburn Rural. He was proud of the tradition-rich tennis programs at Rural. I then knew we were going to try writing this story. And Hedberg, again, assured me that he was nothing special. I think I can find plenty of folks who might share a different opinion about that—lots of perspectives and experiences that might shed light on Hedberg as a person, teacher and coach.

Hurdle one was overcome. Now, the hard stuff. Putting the book in a good, readable format. I already had ideas about how that might look. So, here we go. At this point, it's just a story. We'll see if others think it's book-worthy. Regardless, it will be fun to write.

FOREWORD BY RICK PETERSON

We've probably all heard the phrase: "Nice guys finish last."

But, in a forty-three-year career as a high school teacher and a tennis coach, Kevin Hedberg proved that saying wrong time and time and time again.

Hedberg, who I've had the honor to know for more than three decades, is one of nicest guys I've ever met while also establishing himself as one of the most successful coaches in Kansas high school history.

Hedberg, who retired in the spring of 2022, taught and coached at Washburn Rural for thirty-two years after an eleven-year stint at Seaman—leading the Junior Blues to a Class 6A girls state team title in 1993 and boys state championships in 2003, 2004, 2005 and 2007.

A charter inductee into the Topeka Tennis Association Hall of Fame for his exploits as a player and a coach, Hedberg coached singles and doubles state champions in both boys and girls tennis while coaching twenty-four teams (boys and girls combined) to top-three state team finishes.

But as good as a coach as Hedberg was, he may have been just as good—or better—as a teacher over his long career. And as good as a coach and teacher as Hedberg has been, in my opinion he's an even better man. I'm sure there's somebody our there that doesn't like Kevin Hedberg, but I haven't run across them. Quite frankly, if you don't like Hedberg, it probably tells me more about you than it does about Hedberg.

From the countless students and athletes he worked with—both at Seaman and Washburn Rural—to all the athletes and coaches he faced as an opponent, I believe he earned their universal respect and admiration, willing to lend a hand to anyone that needed it.

As a reporter, the man has always frustrated the heck out of me for the simple fact that it was darn near impossible to get him to say more than a few words about even the loftiest of accomplishments. But, by the same token, Hedberg always had my utmost respect for letting his teams' accomplishments speak for themselves. Those accomplishments, in both the classroom and on the tennis court, speak volumes.

I've long believed that terms like "icon" and "legend" are vastly over-used. However, in the case of Kevin Hedberg, they fit like a glove.

Rick Peterson is a longtime journalist and sports reporter for the Topeka Capital-Journal and current creator and manager of TopSports.news (a new and wonderful media that reports all things sports in Shawnee County in Kansas).

KEVIN HEDBERG'S FORMATIVE YEARS

Hedberg remembers many of his early years spent in western Kansas with his parents. When he was born, his father held a music position in Long Island, Kansas. The town was so small, Hedberg actually was born in the nearby town of Phillipsburg, Kansas. The doctor who assisted with his birth was Dr. Mary Glassen, the first licensed woman doctor in the state.

But the town he remembers most—and most fondly—was in southeast Kansas. Paola. It had a beautiful town square, and it had some tennis options with two local tennis courts.

Both of Kevin's parents were passionate about music and equally enthusiastic about teaching. Kevin's mother, Doris, was a Topeka High and Washburn University graduate who passed away in Topeka in 2021 at the age of ninety-six. A lifelong musician, she sang in many local groups including The Topeka Symphony Chorus in which she was a member for thirty-one years. She was a member of the Shawnee Choral Society and the choir of her church, First United Methodist. She led the children's music choir program at First for twenty-six years. She also taught piano and voice lessons.

Kevin's father, Dr. Floyd "Doc" Carl Hedberg, was also a graduate of Topeka High and Washburn University. He received his master's degree from the University of Kansas and his doctorate from the University of Northern Colorado. He taught music in Long Island and Paola, Kansas before returning to Topeka and Washburn

University where he taught choral music, music education and chaired the department until he retired in 1992. Dr. Hedberg founded the Topeka Symphony Chorus and helped organize the Sunflower Music Festival and its traditions still exist today. Among his many honors, he was selected to the Kansas Music Educators Association's Hall of Fame in 1999.

Floyd Hedberg's music brought him to Paola for a brief stint as a public school music teacher. While there was a ton of musical influence in the family, Kevin remembers his father taking him to the tennis courts where Kevin's father and his father's tennis partner squared off. Kevin was certain he was there to run and shag balls for the duo. The family left Paola when Kevin was in fourth grade.

Hedberg fondly remembers the move to Topeka. He said he grew up near Washburn Park, near 10th and Oakley in a multiracial, multiethnic neighborhood. And sports for kids was everything. He and his friends played basketball, softball, baseball and touch football. Washburn Park also had two tennis courts. How could he resist playing tennis?

Kevin's first tennis racket came as a "gift" from his parents—one he got when his sister graduated from ninth grade. He was jealous of the gift his sister received for her promotion to high school, and he complained until his folks gave in and bought him a five-dollar, wooden Spalding tennis racket. It was black with red on it, and Hedberg added that it was "kind of flashy for the day." Wooden rackets were the thing. The only thing.

The city parks and recreation department sent tennis teachers around to the various parks and they offered cheap lessons for the kids. Hedberg's mother could look out the front door of the family's home and see him playing tennis at the park. Thus, tennis became a part of Hedberg's life and something he took a liking to quickly.

Hedberg's father had been an athlete in his younger days—playing football, basketball and baseball while at Topeka High. Floyd thought tennis was a good chance for his son to learn a sport, but there also was a basketball goal in the driveway, so both sports became interests for Kevin.

Hedberg recollects that his first tennis teacher was Dennis Patterson who made the lessons fun for Kevin and many of his friends. Patterson was also familiar with the tennis culture developing at Hughes Court in Topeka. He steered Kevin to Hughes Courts so he could play with other kids. Hedberg said,"Once I got there (Hughes), I got hooked. You had to prove that you belonged by being there regularly and getting better at the game."

It also provided a new set of friends to complement his neighbor friends. Hedberg remembers, "One guy I met was Fred Esch, and he worked very hard at the game and would play whenever someone wanted to play." He added, "Ultimately, we became rival players. He was a Hayden High School guy and one year older, but we stayed friends." Esch went on to play tennis at Kansas State University.

"I considered the Hughes atmosphere intoxicating," he said, describing his affinity for the newfound sport, "and it (tennis) was fun and pretty cosmopolitan for a town in Kansas."

Kevin met such notable players as the McGraths, the Clark boys and a fellow named Waltz—each of those names carried a lot of tennis ability. They gladly welcomed him into their tennis community. One friend that Hedberg met was Mark Nordstrom who was two years older. The two would eventually end up attending Topeka High School together. When Hedberg was a sophomore, he was Nordstrom's doubles partner while Nordstrom was a senior. For some strange, inexplicable reason at regionals, the duo of Hedberg and Nordstrom got matched up with the other top doubles team in the first round. So two of the best doubles teams in the tournament met first. Unheard of. And Hedberg and Nordstrom dropped that match, sending them home prematurely.

When Hedberg was readying for junior high school at the then Boswell Junior High, he decided to go out for football. First day of practice, Kevin broke and dislocated two of his fingers. He was carrying the football, was tackled, and his fingers unfortunately ended up under the ball. Both his fingers snapped.

Kevin's folks took him to the emergency room. A doctor named Pusitz (and this will date the story) came into the emergency room smoking a cigar. One of Hedberg's fingers went back into place really easily, but the other was bent so badly that his mother almost fainted at the sight.

"If you can stand ten minutes of intense pain," the doctor said, "you can go home tonight."

As a seventh grader, that was something Kevin had to think about. His father asked, "Ten minutes?" He wasn't going to tell his son what to do.

The doctor backed off the time frame a little and said, "Maybe three or four minutes of pain."

Kevin said he "moxied" up and decided he wanted to try avoiding a night's stay in the hospital. He preferred to be home.

The doctor took hold of Kevin's finger and counted, "One, two,..." and then he pulled the finger out and stuck it back in. About two seconds worth of time. He resumed smoking his cigar, and all was well. Except for the fact that Kevin had to wear a splint on his fingers and was out of football for many days.

As a result of Hedberg missing so many of the football practices—and given that, then, the practices truly were for initial skill development—Kevin talked to his father and decided not to continue football. In those days, junior high was a young boy's first exposure to football. Hedberg knew he was going to fall way behind when he couldn't practice with the other boys. He simply waited for basketball season since he knew he was good enough to play basketball.

Later that same spring, he also went out for the junior high tennis team. And there he found quite early on that he was the best player at his school. At that time, there may have been eleven junior high schools in the urban Topeka USD 501 school district. They competed against each other in sports. Not every school had a tennis team, but it was good competition.

Hedberg spoke well of his coaches. He had a basketball coach his seventh-grade year named George Quinderas who was gruff and demanding, but really fair. According to Hedberg, his most influential coach as a freshman was Bob Hays—not because of his X's and O's as much as his positive influence on Kevin and the kids he coached. I myself had the opportunity to work with Hays when we were fellow athletic directors in the Centennial League. I always enjoyed working out scheduling issues with Bob. He knew we both tried to come up with a win-win scenario.

I caught up with Bob Hays and asked him about his recollections of Kevin Hedberg, both as a student and now as an adult. Hays indicated that Hedberg was a student of his at Boswell Junior High School in 1967. Bob got to know him as a student in his physical education class and a member of the basketball team. Hays remembered, "Kevin was a young man who was mature far beyond his years. He was one of those students that you would like to see replicated into a whole classroom (of students). Kevin was such a neat young man, a good student, and one who cared about how he presented himself to others."

Educators have a tendency to remember many of their students, but some stand out a little more than others. Hays said, "I could tell by the kind of young man he was in junior high that he was going to do well in whatever endeavor he undertook in the future. As I followed his successes at Washburn Rural High School, it certainly confirmed my thoughts." Some kids are unpredictable. Then there are the Kevin Hedbergs, and you see the traits of a very capable future adult very early in their development."

As the two parted ways and Kevin went to Topeka High School, Hays remembers a time when they reconnected. "We ran into each other occasionally over the years. A couple of instances stand out in my mind. One evening I was in the stands watching a Topeka High basketball game, and Kevin was a high school student at Topeka High. He saw me and made the effort to come and sit with me to talk about the game and to just carry on a general conversation." Now that their relationship was on the peripheral rather than teacher/student, Hays fondly recalled the interaction saying, "It was as if I was talking to a friend. It always makes a teacher and coach feel good when one of their former students takes the time to converse with them."

The second interaction occurred while Hays was attending a track meet at Washburn Rural. He had parked his vehicle near the tennis courts where Hedberg was practicing with his team. "As I left the track meet and headed to my car," Hays remembers, "I saw Kevin. I went onto the tennis courts and said 'Hi' to him. Kevin came over and invited me to come onto the courts and meet his son who was on the tennis team that year. That was a great experience. It made me feel special that he wanted me to meet his son. We visited for a few minutes, and I headed out so he could continue practice. It was always great to see him."

That's the way Hedberg leaves lots of folks feeling after interacting with him. He acts as though what you have to say is really important to him. I wonder if that is one of the reasons kids relate so well to him? Most often, the majority of kids always did connect with him.

In Hedberg's ninth-grade year, he won the Topeka city singles championship. He hadn't won it his seventh or eighth grade years. There was a very good tennis athlete named Mark Jensen who had gone undefeated all the way through junior high until Kevin beat him at the city meet. The week before the city tournament, Jensen beat Hedberg 9-7. Hedberg said Jensen was a better golfer than a tennis player, and he chose to participate in golf in high school.

Hedberg also played basketball through his sophomore year at Topeka High. It was there, during that year, he learned a valuable lesson about commitment. Kevin was a member of the student council at the time. Back in the day, various Kansas high school student councils liked to have exchanges with other schools. It was the second week of January, and Wichita Southeast wanted to do an exchange. Hedberg was a starting guard on the sophomore basketball team. In order to go on the exchange, he would have to miss a week of basketball practice and two games. His coach at the time, Don Bliss, was very fair according to Hedberg. The only question Bliss posed to Hedberg before he left school for the exchange was, "This is really important to you?" Hedberg told him it was, and he participated in the exchange.

When he came back, he had lost his starting role on the basketball team and never started again. Hedberg said he knew that what Coach Bliss was really trying to convey and wanted him to think about was that, apparently, his role on the team was not as important as the student council event. The lesson was: just how important was it to be a part of this basketball team?

At that time, there was a real sense of community at the Hughes tennis courts. That's where Kevin developed his friend base. When they weren't playing tennis, they were playing cards or wiffle ball, and they played football at Gage Park. The Hughes crew were all really, really competitive with each other. And it really pushed all of them to work hard.

Hedberg met Mark Nordstrom—who was two years older than him—through the Hughes tennis community, and they quickly became good friends in high school.

They remain good friends today. Topeka tennis was really competitive. According to Hedberg, Highland Park had good tennis teams as did Topeka High. Topeka West was a relatively new school. But all the Topeka tennis players knew each other well through their association at Hughes Courts where they all learned tennis and played there together.

John Waltz became a good rival for Hedberg in high school. Hedberg got the best of Waltz in junior high, but when they played in high school matches, it was about 50-50 as to who won.

When Hedberg was fifteen, he started entering Missouri Valley tennis competitions and traveled to compete. He admitted that he immediately thought he was a lot better than he really was though he did experience some success. When he came home, he remembers entering a local tournament and losing to a young man who he had never lost to. He was down on the back courts when he lost, and he was infuriated. He hated to lose, especially when he felt he should have won. Hedberg said he kicked his racket all the way to the upper courts and was saying the "F-word" as he made the ascent. His kicking and cursing did not go unnoticed.

About six weeks later, he got a letter from the Missouri Valley Tennis Association that said, "If your behavior doesn't change, we are going to ban you from the sport for two years." That upcoming weekend, he was already entered in a big tournament in Ark City, Kansas. He was going to play age 16-18 boys singles. His father sat him down with the letter and said, "This is it. I'm going to go ahead and send you, you're already paid for, but this is it. You've got to change."

Hedberg went to the tournament and put on his best behavior. He actually won the sportsmanship award that they gave out at the conclusion of the event, and he had a great tournament. That experience changed him in a big way. He was convinced that, to play better tennis, he had to focus on how he competed instead of whether he won. From then on, he was a gentleman on the courts and, because of his demeanor, knows he played so much better. A valuable life lesson that Hedberg lived by was not to be so focused on THE WIN. From then on, he became a competitor. And that's what he tried to instill in the players he later coached and mentored.

Hedberg had fond memories of being a seventeen-year old and playing in his first Hutchinson Open. It was common back then for the competitors to travel to a tournament and stay at the homes of tournament patrons. Hedberg remembers his first visit and the first family who put him up in their home. The Spencers. Also, Hedberg remembered the name of the player who defeated him. Van Thompson was a familiar name in tennis back then. And Hedberg likely remembers that, eight years later, he got his revenge against Thompson—defeating him in the Topeka Jayhawk Open.

Hutch tennis players followed Hedberg wherever he played. As a junior in high school, Hedberg finished fourth in the state tournament and finished third as a senior. Randy Fletchall of Hutch was his consolation round victim, while Pat Hays of Hutch beat him in the semifinals.

At age thirty-three, Hedberg continued to return to tournaments he won as a youth. And as age crept up on him, so did the younger, more youthful players. He won tournaments as a young player and remembers when he considered himself in the middle of the field of the competitors statewide. He was used to being at the top of competition. Inevitably, age always beats us.

Who did Hedberg admire in the realm of professional tennis? He recollects that, as a young man, he admired John Newcombe "and the other Aussies." He also admired Arthur Ashe on the national level. "I really admired some of the regional players as well, like Jim Burns (Kansas University tennis coach), Van Thompson at Wichita State." And bringing it to the more modern players, he mentioned Sampras, Federer and Nadal because of their consistent excellence and also for the way they respect the game of tennis.

PICKING A COLLEGE TO ATTEND

Nowadays, it seems that one of the most arduous decisions a high school senior, who is also an athlete, makes is where to pursue their post-secondary education. If athletics or activities are going to be a part of their experience, they carefully weigh everything involved in their choice of schools. Many agonize over the decision, the choices presented to them.

Kevin Hedberg finished high school and had enough success as a high school tennis player that three of the best state universities came calling for him to attend college and play for their tennis teams.

Hedberg had an offer from Kansas State University, University of Kansas and Washburn University. And, as Hedberg put it, each school had plenty of scholarship money in the early '70s. Each of them offered a full ride. During Hedberg's years, Washburn may have been on an even keel, competitively, with KU. Kansas State had probably the best tennis team at the time.

At the time, Hedberg weighed the following: He had a good friend from high school at Washburn—Nordstrom, who he had played doubles with while in high school—and George Parker was Nordstrom's tennis coach at Washburn and was a good gentleman. I also got to know Coach Parker from my days as an Ichabod where I took physical education classes from him. He was old school. An extremely judicious person. Parker's positive influence and examples were passed on to a lot of future physical education teachers studying at Washburn University during his tenure.

Kansas State University had a very good tennis program at the time, so that was appealing to Hedberg as well.

Another factor involved in his choice of schools was that Hedberg had played KU's number one tennis player multiple times at various tournaments. Kevin had won those matches, so he felt he could compete for KU's number one spot as an incoming college freshman.

He was patiently weighing those offers. He had letters of intent. One had to be signed by August 1. In early July, he felt like he had made his decision and was going to commit to KU. He liked the school as well as the tennis program and its coach. At about the same time he had come to a decision, the KU coach he thought so much of contacted him to say he was leaving the University to accept a job in Arizona. This coach recommended he wait on his school commitment to see who KU hired because the coach is possibly one of the most important factors in one's decision about what school to attend. If you're going to spend that much time in a sport, you had better like working for the coach you will play for.

The University of Kansas kept dragging their feet on a new hire, and when South Florida threw their hat in the ring as a possible school for Hedberg to attend, he contacted a Topekan named Harold Kossover for advice about what he ought to do. Hedberg called Kossover a mentor—someone who he would go to for advice. Kossover's brother was a tennis coach in Arkansas. They were a well-known Topeka tennis family whose name would eventually be attached to the Kossover tennis complex near 25th and Gage. Also, at the time, there was a former Topeka High school administrator, Charles "Chick" Gordon, who had left High for a college teaching position at South Florida. South Florida had started offering a teacher's educational program, and Gordon was part of the Florida school's faculty.

At this time, Hedberg was working at the Topeka putt putt facility located near 21st and Belle. One night, while on duty, the pay phone rang, and it was South Florida. Back in the day, the business phone of the putt putt facility WAS the pay phone. The South Florida coach said that the number one high school graduate from Colorado, who previously had committed to attend South Florida, had just backed out of his scholarship. The coach told Hedberg that the scholarship was his if he wanted it. The one stipulation was that four years of his school would be funded IF Hedberg could make the team as one of the top six players in his first year there. Hedberg knew he would have had a good career and a good time at any of the three Kansas colleges, but he opted for Florida. When I asked him how he had felt secure enough about passing up a sure scholarship in Kansas to choose having to earn one in Florida, he said, "I was cocky." He was definitely confident in his abilities.

Kevin's feelings were that, as a community and a state, most folks don't often think of Kansas tennis with the proper respect. He talked about the Kansas tennis player who beat him seven times in high school and also won the Kansas state championship who then went to Arizona State where he played singles and was an All-American. The guy who finished second at the same high school state tournament beat Hedberg in the semifinals. This same player had also beaten the state champion earlier in the year and was undefeated when he played Hedberg. This young man went to Iowa University on a full-ride scholarship. So Kansas tennis players knew they could compete with just about anyone, any college, any state. There will be more about the strength of Kansas tennis in the book. Hedberg has strong, calculated, valid and convincing opinions to support the premise that Kansas tennis was and is at an elite level.

When considering the prospects of attending South Florida, Hedberg and his father punched the calculator. The most significant difference was the cost of flying home and the return flights to Tampa. Hedberg said that he was surprised that his father was willing to put him on a plane—for the first time—and send him so far away to school. But as he reflected on this later, his dad was likely not paralyzed by a challenge. After all, at age nineteen, his father served in the military and was in Okinawa. That certainly had to be a far bigger challenge for any young man.

So in September, Hedberg boarded Braniff Airways at old Kansas City Municipal Airport with his meager belongings which included his tennis rackets. It was the first airplane flight of his young life. He had ten dollars in his pocket. He changed planes in Dallas and, thanks to the help of a friendly businessman on his flight, he was able to catch the connecting flight to Tampa. Once he arrived in Florida, he was supposed to meet Gordon and the South Florida tennis coach at the airport. Problem was, he was at the Braniff baggage claim. They were at the TWA baggage claim. No cell phones in those days, so Hedberg correctly ascertained that he was on his own getting himself to the South Florida campus.

He flagged down a cab and matter-of-factly told the driver where he wanted to get, but also told him he only had ten dollars. The cab driver told him that amount of cash would get him within about four miles of South Florida's campus. Hedberg told him that was better than where he was now and took the cab ride. He got distracted on the drive and the cabbie ended up dropping him off at his dormitory. When Hedberg offered him the ten, the driver told him to keep it. "You need it worse than I do," the generous cabbie said.

Thus began Hedberg's ascension into the University of South Florida. With ten dollars in his pocket and the uncertainty of whether he would earn a scholarship, Hedberg was safely on the campus. Now it was up to him and his tennis playing abilities to earn that scholarship.

Hedberg had lots of good things to say about his South Florida coach, Spafford Taylor. Spaff, as he was called, was a tremendous athlete who played college football at Georgia (later the 2022 and 2023 national champion Georgia Bulldogs). The guy was an All-American defensive back at Georgia. Initially, Taylor was not really a tennis guy. He was a physical education guy who eventually learned what he needed to know about tennis and willed himself to be a good tennis player as well. He became proficient enough that he spent his summers as a tennis pro at a facility in Ashville, North Carolina. As a person and coach, Hedberg said Taylor was always concerned about the welfare of his players. Kevin called him "a good spiritual man." Unfortunately, Taylor passed away in the fall of 2022 at the writing of this book. He was ninety-four. I would say, in many instances, the mentors we have when we are younger provide us with part of the blueprint that helps us do the work we do.

According to his obituary Spafford Taylor also served his country in the Army prior to joining the physical education department at the University of South Florida in 1964. He remained at the university until 1974. His final year coaching was Hedberg's senior season when the team went 21-3 and finished 25th in the NCAA Division 1 tournament.

What Taylor did for his tennis players, to give them a tremendous advantage over other teams, was focus on their fitness. They began every practice with a three-mile run before they ever set foot on the tennis courts. After two-hours of hitting on the courts and practicing their tennis strokes and volleys, they made their way to a sand dune that was located in the middle of the campus. This dune was about fifty feet high according to Hedberg. They sprinted up and down that sand dune again and again. What else does a tennis player need besides good endurance and strong legs? They already had very good tennis skills. This was at a time when fitness was not as much of a priority, nor was strength training. Back in the day, many coaches discouraged weights and swimming because they wanted tennis players' muscles to be loose and long. Much like baseball pitchers.

Teams from up north in the Big Ten would come down to Florida for matches in the spring. The temperatures in Tampa would be in the 80s and, because of the fitness of the South Florida players, they just wore out the visitors and beat them in the long tennis matches in part due to their superior endurance. Hedberg said that Taylor was well ahead of his time focusing so much on conditioning. And it paid dividends.

When Hedberg was a senior, there was an article in the Tampa Tribune by sportswriter Greg Gordon titled, "Hedberg And USF: Good For Each Other." In the article, Gordon talks about Hedberg's decision to attend USF and also spoke of his ascent as a player during his time there. Gordon described the decision as a "lucky" one for the tennis program.

In that article he talks about Hedberg having options to attend three Kansas colleges. He says Hedberg became aware of the school in Tampa his junior year in high school from a pamphlet he was given. And, as luck would have it, when Hedberg was a senior, Coach Taylor's attempt to get two Colorado teammates to attend USF fell through. This opened the door for Hedberg.

The article also mentions that, as a freshman, Hedberg played as the number four singles player and posted a dual match record of 10-11 and then, as a sophomore, he went 11-11 as a number two singles player. As a junior, he played number one singles and, at five feet eight inches and one hundred and fifty pounds, finished 14-11 in dual matches against his opponents' best players. At the time of this particular article's writing, his senior season record was 7-3.

Hedberg said in the article, "At the beginning (of the year), I felt some pressures," regarding playing number one singles as a junior, "but you get used to having a crowd and knowing that you'll play the best player on the other team."

The article mentioned his first ten matches as a junior. He started off 3-7 before reeling off the next eleven wins out of his fifteen matches to end the year at a respectable 14-11 mark.

The Tampa reporter, Gordon, also said Kevin's best victory was a 6-1, 6-1 win over Rollin Rob Bradley to which Hedberg admitted that he had played so well, his opponent didn't have a chance. The biggest win of his collegiate career came on their road trip the last year when they met Mississippi State. Hedberg faced Canada's fifth-ranked player in Jim Boyce and beat him 6-4, 1-6, 6-4.

After his junior year campaign, Hedberg was eagerly looking ahead to his senior year. He mentioned that he had seen so many tennis players burn out by their senior year, and he didn't want that to happen to him. Unfortunately, Hedberg suffered a back injury in May, which kept him from actually playing until the end of September of his senior year. He also had an operation to remove a node on his racket arm, and it caused concern that injuries might preempt or end his collegiate career prematurely. They didn't, and, as the only senior on the team, he played the most solid number three singles in the school's history. Hedberg told Gordon, "At first I thought I'd smash people playing number three, but it doesn't work that way."

Coach Taylor commented, "He (Hedberg) found out that you do get the tough players at the third position and he took some losses which he shouldn't have." Taylor went on to say, "He's playing tough now like he was at this time last year."

Taylor had additional compliments to dish out saying, "He's improved his overall game. He's not a jumping, jerky player like he was. He's smoothed out his strokes and is thinking better and is more thoughtful about his shots and prior to the match he prepares himself for what he's going to do."

Being the only fourth-year player, "Kevin is in a position where, as a senior, it's been pressed upon him that you're expected to do more and live up to the responsibility.

"He puts himself last and his obligation to the team first and he's always been a hard worker and a team man. When he was forced to play at the number one position last year, he took the responsibility and came out with a winning record on the toughest schedule we have ever had."

Taylor said that in the four years Kevin played for USF he had never heard any negative remarks from other coaches, or from his teammates. "His leadership qualities came out the last two years, " the coach shared, "and there's no doubt that the rest of the guys look up to Kevin. Kevin has measured up in a model form and I just hope he's gained something from being here."

The reporter wrote that "the future of Kevin Hedberg is still uncertain although he definitely wants to stay in the tennis profession for as long as he can. He has applied for a job at a new tennis complex (Topeka Country Club) in Topeka, but hasn't heard from them yet."

In the article, Hedberg admitted one regret that he had about coming to Florida—it was just so far from his home. "My parents never saw me play in the four years I've been here. They've done so much to put me down here, I'd just like to play for them and give them an opportunity to see me play."

The article ended with the reporter saying this, "That's just the way Kevin Hedberg is, obligations first, himself last." I'd say that was a pretty accurate statement then and now.

Kevin Hedberg always had an interest in history, and because of this, he was motivated to learn and study it. Despite the rigors of collegiate sports participation, he was able to earn his degree in four years. His bachelor's degree was in history, which included the social studies spectrum.

As is the case with some majors of study, this degree would require some additional schooling to gain a path into a marketable job. What would Kevin do after college?

The newly hired coach at South Florida who would replace Kevin's coach asked him to stay on and help him coach as a graduate assistant. However, Kevin found another option that would allow him to work, pay living expenses AND continue his love of playing tennis and competing. He accepted a job in his hometown at the Topeka Country Club overseeing their tennis offerings.

HEDBERG EARNS HIS COLLEGE DEGREE— CONTINUES TO PLAY TENNIS COMPETITIVELY

When Hedberg was working at a tennis club in Houston, he often returned to Topeka to play in numerous tennis events. In a Memorial Day tournament at Hughes Tennis Courts, Hedberg defeated John Runnels. Runnels was leading Hedberg 4-2 in a nine-point tie breaker that would determine the set—one Runnels needed since Hedberg had won the first set 6-4. Runnels' plan was to continue to pressure Hedberg, and he decided to come up on Hedberg's serve. It didn't work. Hedberg won the next three points and the tiebreaker, giving him the second set 7-6 and the match.

The nineteen-year old Runnels told Mark Nusbaum, then a Capital-Journal newspaper sportswriter, that, "I really felt like I was doing what I wanted to do on those last three points." Runnels had also lost the July 4th tennis Tournament to Hedberg the previous year 7-5, 6-4. Runnels said, "It was just one of those things. He hit some good shots, and I just couldn't come up with the one I needed."

Hedberg continued his dominance of local Topeka tennis as he also won the initial Capital City Open in the summer of 1981. This meet replaced the traditional Labor Day Tennis tournament that Hedberg had won before. And once again, Hedberg had to defeat an up-and-coming young tennis player, O.J. Thomas, in the finals 6-4, 6-3.

"We had a lot of good points," Hedberg said. Both Thomas and Hedberg were Topeka High graduates. "O.J was hitting the ball really well. It just made me remember how good he really was when he was a junior," Hedberg added. "If Joel Hoffman hadn't been around, he (Thomas) would have been the standout among the city juniors."

Hoffman went on to play at the University of Houston and then joined the Penn Tennis Circuit.

Always the gentleman competitor, Hedberg mentioned, "His (Thomas') game is really effective on these courts, too. He can stay back and hit well enough to win points."

In Nusbaum's newspaper article, he mentioned that Hedberg was "a little too strong" for the younger Runnels. There are some perks that come with age. One is having your good friend write articles about you in the local newspaper.

HEDBERG FORGOES THE TENNIS CLUB LIFE FOR TEACHING AND COACHING— THE SEAMAN HIGH SCHOOL YEARS (1980-1991)

I asked Hedberg why he eventually chose to be an educator and a coach. Of course he had a big influence at home. His dad was a teacher. He then had the good fortune to be taught, coached and mentored by some fine educators. He mentioned Bob Hays. Larry Reid, Mr. Peck, his ninth grade coach, and Don Bliss.

"I had always thought about it (teaching as a career). In college I was so intent on playing tennis that I wanted a degree and a major I could complete rather easily," Hedberg reflected. "History was a natural for me since I read so much as a child."

But tennis was his plan. "I really planned on working/playing tennis after college," Hedberg confessed. "My first three years at Topeka Country Club were fun, but not lucrative." He then moved to Houston for a year, but came back to Kansas City, specifically the Overland Park area. It was there that Hedberg discovered something.

"I enjoyed teaching kids, but not adults," Hedberg recalled. He mentioned that he did not enjoy "serving adults." It was at this point he made the conscious decision to try teaching. Our previous experiences do influence us in our career choices.

He moved back to Topeka and ended up completing the educational methods courses at Washburn University, the ones necessary to be able to earn his teaching degree and certification. His first exposure to the classroom was his student teaching experience at Seaman High School. That experience led to his first teaching and coaching assignment, which was also at Seaman.

In his first year, he was making the transition from country club pro to teacher and high school coach. He told Capital-Journal sportswriter Karen Sipes, "I like it (coaching), but it's a lot different. I thought I knew it all, but I didn't. When I got to the first couple of tennis meets, I realized I had a lot to learn. The most difficult thing about it is that you have to know where to start and where to attack." And he mentioned he was also becoming familiar with "the team situation (for high school tennis) and how to bring them along. When teaching private lessons, you didn't have to worry about any of that."

He also learned that, while it helps to have been a winner himself in tennis competitions, it was not that big a factor when coaching high school kids. "I have won a lot of tournaments and I have a good record, but to the girls high school tennis players at Seaman, I am just another coach. You get used to having people hang on what you are saying (as a pro), and then you find you have to tell the members on your team three or four times what you want them to do."

Another adjustment from the tennis pro at a private club to a teacher/coach is the small amount of compensation paid to teachers. "I took the route (of pro) for the money in a hurry. That is a world where you get paid for almost everything, then you walk into education and that is a world of sacrifice. I almost feel guilty leaving practice at a quarter to five and the football team is out there working. The one thing that strikes me most about it is the degree of dedication of the coaches (in all other sports). Just seeing them has been really good for me."

That first year, Hedberg found out that there are other ways to be rewarded than simply monetarily. When he watched his first Seaman girls team finish third in its league tournament and realized how much they had improved, he said, "I never dreamed at the beginning of the season that we would do that well." Also, his top singles player, Paige Ruedlinger, won the Centennial League singles championship.

Ruedlinger told local Capital-Journal sports reporter Sipes, "I think what did it was getting such a good coach." That's a compliment those pricey tennis lessons can't buy you. That gratification is priceless to high school coaches. To teachers, a "thank you" means a lot. It means you've had some degree of success, and you've obviously affected your players' character as well when they dish out that kind of praise and acknowledge your efforts on their behalf.

"I had a lot of great experiences at Seaman. The job kept me from going over the edge when my first wife divorced me. The coaching of both teams (girls and boys) was enjoyable and challenging." Hedberg remembers that, in his earliest days at Seaman, he would likely have two or three kids that could play tennis somewhat well. So the job required building a program. Seaman had a developmental summer program that Hedberg took over and taught and, as the number of tennis players grew, so did the quality of the Seaman tennis program. Eventually, the teams became competitive with the other city and league schools.

"The kids over there (Seaman is north of Topeka) were great kids." And, with the social studies classes he taught there, he ended up teaching every graduate of Seaman in those days.

As the tennis got better, Hedberg recalls, "My girls teams, by the mid 1980s were legit, not league champs, but we began to qualify individuals and teams for the state tournament most years. And the boys teams followed suit and, in 1985, we tied Washburn Rural for the Centennial League championship." What was rewarding for him to watch was that the kids now playing for Seaman were mostly products of his summer programs. "So that was greatly satisfying." To this day, that '85 league title is Seaman's only one in boys tennis.

Hedberg recalls fondly his time at Seaman. He is proud of the fact that several of the Seaman High School boys were able to go on and play tennis at the college level. He mentioned Randy Evans, Rik Evans and Chris McAbee. McAbee took fourth in state singles as a senior. And on the girls side, he had two who played in college.

Calla Yingling played locally at Washburn. Beck McAbee attended and played at Johnson County Community College. It's funny how the pipelines get started and sustain themselves as other players aspire to do the same.

Hedberg also valued the relationships he made with colleagues at Seaman. He mentioned Brad Dietz, Ron Vinduska, Bob Karr and Bill Annan who came to Washburn Rural to teach business and coach girls basketball the same year Hedberg did. A couple of his dad's friends from his Topeka High school days also taught at Seaman—Blackie Melvin and Tom Carlson.

"My worst experience there was leaving. I had to tell Amelia Holmes, Mark Riddle and Wade Sloan (students) that I would not be there for their senior year, and I really loved those kids." Teachers hate goodbyes. After all, you build relationships intending to stay and see them graduate.

Another challenge was having to tell his principal. Hedberg remembers it well. "Walking into Don Pierce's office to tell him I was leaving was one of the hardest things I ever did." Hedberg says he had so much respect for Pierce. The fact that Pierce had hired him for his first teaching and coaching position was compounded by the fact that he loved it at Seaman. That made leaving that much more difficult for him.

"I have been blessed by working under principals that were excellent. Don Pierce ran a tight ship," he remembers, "but I loved it. If you messed up, he came directly to you and and let you know, cleared the air and set the expectation. It only happened to me once, and it was somewhat trivial. It was an offhand comment I made in class, but it never happened again." And Hedberg was honest in his confession when he mentioned, "That is not to say I always agreed with administrator decisions, but I respected him, so I knew he had legitimate reasons when he acted."

I thought it would be interesting—since I didn't know much about Kevin when he was at Seaman, just knew who he was—to get some personal experiences and stories from former colleagues and former students.

Kevin was ingrained as a Seaman High teacher by 1985 when Susan Sittenauer joined the Seaman faculty as a new teacher. Susan was also a social studies teacher. She remembers meeting Hedberg in the fall of that first year she taught and knew him as a person who was "warm and friendly." In her first week on the job, the Seaman Board of Education added the position of assistant girls tennis coach for the program. Kevin approached her and asked if she'd consider being his assistant tennis coach. Her question was simple, "Do I have to know anything about tennis?" As the position was assistant girls coach, Kevin's reply was, "No, just hand the girls tampons when they need them, and give them a shoulder to cry on when they are upset." That was a little indicative of Hedberg's propensity to joke and jest. Sittenauer told Hedberg she could do that, and she ended up being the assistant tennis coach for the Seaman girls program for nine years.

As Sittenauer reflected on the role Hedberg played as a staff member at Seaman, she mentioned, "Kevin was the person that the Seaman staff went to when they had a question or there was a conflict and they needed sound, common sense advice." According to Sittenauer, Hedberg had his own unique approach to problem solving which included "a quick wit" but also followed by providing "a measured and reasonable solution to any situation that arose."

She went on to say, "All of the staff had a great respect for Kevin. He was very well liked. He had a sharp wit and a great sense of humor." From her own personal experience, she said, "As a brand new teacher, I felt fortunate to have had his guiding influence." Hedberg was an excellent mentor to so many on and off the tennis courts.

As competent as Hedberg was with teaching tennis skills, he also recognized that there was a human side to coaching. He also knew how valuable it could be having a female to assist him with the female student-athletes. He could coach the daily practice and tennis skills needed, but valued the support a female assistant could provide the athletes. Physically and emotionally, a woman's touch was extremely valuable, and Hedberg prioritized that over having someone who would be another tennis technician.

Having the close association with Hedberg working side by side, Sittenauer also got a taste of what made him so successful. She reflected, "Kevin is brilliant with regard to motivating his players, and the fact that he can actually play well can therefore be a role model." Combining his motivation with his skills to demonstrate, "He was able to raise their level of play. He knows when to be real and somewhat tough and when to show compassion. He recognizes that it is sometimes a fine line between the two."

Sittenauer herself has become a respected teacher and became the current head of the social studies department when I spoke to her in 2021. What she received from Kevin was invaluable. "Kevin was such a strong mentor for me as a novice teacher. I don't know if I would have survived my first three to four years of teaching without his having my back and looking out fo me." Sittenauer went on to say, "He gave me so much incredible advice and was always a positive force. I was a complete rookie and I needed a veteran to help me navigate how to become an effective teacher."

And as a teacher myself, I remember the influences in my initial years and how important those experienced teachers were to my development as an effective teacher. So many good mentors who gave me real-time instructional hints and techniques. Knowing Kevin and having seen these qualities myself for thirty years at Washburn Rural, it simply reinforced what I already knew about him. Kevin is the kind of person who recognizes that his job is much more enjoyable if the overall school climate is positive, and he worked diligently to improve and influence that environment. Students benefited directly and indirectly from Hedberg. His influence can truly help shape the climate of your school. People, kids especially, trust Kevin Hedberg. They listen to him.

Another social studies teacher that shared classroom time with Hedberg was Ron Vinduska. Vinduska eventually became the principal of Seaman High School. I had the privilege of working with Vinduska when he was Seaman's athletic director and while he was the school's principal. We worked well together and closely while serving each of our schools. Ron was easy to work with. He learned how to protect the interests of his school while also being flexible when considering our school's needs. I never recall a matter that we couldn't compromise on and work out. Brad Dietz replaced Ron as the athletic director, and we had a similar good working relationship. More importantly, I counted them as friends. Hedberg felt the same way about the two.

Vinduska recollects the time when he and Hedberg both taught in the social studies department together. His recollection of Hedberg is an instructor with a "calm, easy-going style that made him much more cool than I'd ever be." That may be one of the most spot-on descriptions of Hedberg's classroom demeanor. Cool and confident. Students were interested in what he had to say, what he was teaching them. Hedberg was interesting no matter what the topic of discussion happened to be or what the lecture related to. He made it relevant to kids.

In addition to "cool," Vinduska mentioned, "He is outstanding in the classroom and was able to relate to all types of kids." Vinduska taught the Honors American History students, and Hedberg taught the regular kids. "We all knew that his students would always be challenged and have a great learning experience."

Something that helped Hedberg with his relationships with students was his sense of humor. He became a prankster among his colleagues and fellow teachers. To liven up the work environment at Seaman—which was a bit non-traditional with an open classroom concept—the teachers shared a private work space in a shared teacher workroom. According to Vinduska, things would magically appear or disappear with a note signed "The Phantom." Everyone suspected that Hedberg was behind the mystery disappearances and notes, although Hedberg never admitted it. Vinduska went on to say,"It was a great way to keep staff loose and not take oneself to seriously."

But one of Vinduska's—and I'm certain many other Seaman staff members'—most fond recollections had to do with their principal's end-of-the-year process of gathering grade cards of students who owed money for obligations unfulfilled. It might be a student-athlete out for sports who failed to turn in their uniform or equipment. The principal at Seaman at the time was the highly popular and well-respected Don Pierce. Pierce's process involved all the teachers meeting in the library. Pierce would have the obligation list that the teachers helped make—a list of what student-athlete owed what. And Pierce would read off the student names from the obligation list. Each teacher would hand that kid's grade card to him to be held in the principal's office until the obligation was met.

According to Vinduska, the teachers were not fond of the process. Most of them felt like there had to be a better way to deal with delinquent obligations other than holding grade cards. Students who didn't perform well were likely happy to not take their grade cards home if they had less than a good grade.

On one particular collection day, Pierce was working his way through the obligation list when he called out, "Richard Nibbler." There was a long pause because no teacher had Nibbler's grade card(s). So Pierce called "Richard Nibbler" again with a little more volume and urgency. And, again, no one had the grade cards. A few of the teachers began to sense what was occurring, so a few smiles started to appear on the staff's faces. The obligation explanation said that the kid owed Hedberg a book. Finally Pierce bellowed, "Doesn't anyone have a Richard Nibbler in class? Hedberg sheepishly raised his hand and said, "Maybe he goes by Dick Nibbler?" Then the "light" went on in Pierce's brain, and he actually cracked a smile, which, according to Vinduska, was rare. Eventually, he moved away from calling for the fictitious Dick Nibbler. Nobody dared laugh in front of Don Pierce, but it came later when the faculty shared some time together. Of course Hedberg was the suspect since he had created the "student's" obligation.

In addition to adding some comic relief to the stressful job of teaching, Vinduska also says, "Kevin was always a friend you could trust." Vinduska reflected on his personal experience with Hedberg. "One year we (he and Hedberg) had the same plan period, and we'd jog on the track during the hour. I had some personal issues that spring, and I remember confiding in Kevin about some of the stuff going on in my life. He was a great person to bounce ideas off of. I knew he'd never breathe a word of anything we shared to anyone. He was trustworthy."

Professionally, the two worked on Seaman's social studies Northcentral School Accreditation for the social studies department, and he mentioned that Hedberg always did a good, thorough job even though there were times they failed to see the importance of the tasks or the relevance. We teachers from that period of time can relate to that innocuous process so well.

And with Hedberg, there was always tennis. Vinduska's observation was that the biggest challenge with the Seaman kids was to convince players to work on tennis in the off season and to believe that if they worked, listened, and took it seriously, they could compete with the best in the city. Vinduska was happy to say, "Eventually that happened, and our team became much more competitive and less recreational." Hedberg pushed that agenda every day and in every way while he worked at Seaman High School.

Hedberg mentioned that he had gotten close to some Seaman kids who were going to be seniors. He had to let those kids know that he was switching jobs and leaving Seaman, and he said it was one of the most difficult parts associated with his changing jobs, changing schools.

His top two boys players heading into their senior years were Mark Riddle and Wade Sloan. According to Sloan, they both had become extremely close with Hedberg. He recollected a summer when Hedberg's wife moved her downtown law office to another location, and the two tennis players helped the coach.

Since their freshman year, both young men spent countless hours on the Seaman tennis courts honing their own tennis skills. Additionally, they both helped with Hedberg's summer camps. But it was the time spent with their coach driving to high school matches that gave them that special connection with Hedberg.

"Mark and I went on lots of road trips in that big ugly tan Seaman High School station wagon," Sloan recalls, "to matches around town and around the state." He mentioned that he never had Hedberg as a classroom teacher, "but I know everyone in school hoped to get in his class because he was the coolest and funniest teacher in school. We (he and Riddle) felt pretty lucky that we got to spend so much time with him, and I think most students were envious we got to spend so much time with him and be so close with him."

As so often happens in school situations, Sloan remembers he and Riddle getting called to one of the Seaman conference rooms. They thought it was weird and unusual, but had no idea what they were about to hear. In fact, Sloan said he wondered, "was I in some sort of trouble even though I didn't know why?"

Hedberg was in the conference room waiting to speak to them about his decision to leave Seaman and join the Washburn Rural High School faculty. "I really don't remember much of what was said," Sloan recalled, "other than he told us he had made the decision to go to Washburn Rural. I think we were pretty quiet and said we understood, but we were shocked. We never anticipated him leaving. I doubt I said much because I was probably worried about crying in front of Coach and Mark. I'm sure I was fighting it back."

As young students, it likely was hard to comprehend the reasons associated with the move and maybe not all contributing reasons were shared. So, Sloan eventually assumed, in part, that it was a great opportunity for Hedberg. As a young high school student, his perception was that facilities and money may have been better at Rural. Since I was the Athletic Director at Rural, I can tell you that the money was likely not a big factor. Salary schedules and coaches supplemental contracts were pretty similar across the city. We did expand our courts, but eventually so did Seaman. I doubt that Hedberg delved into the family stuff that prompted his move—the part about him wanting to be more involved in his daughter's middle and high school years to help keep her on the straight and narrow. A conscientious Hedberg would not want to lay that much on a young kid to have to think about.

Although Sloan said they missed Hedberg being their coach their senior year, he mentioned that they had a great year, tennis wise, and had a blast.

One fond recollection of Hedberg oddly came during the winter basketball awards banquet. Then basketball coach, Brad Dietz, was presenting Sloan with his all-city recognition along with his all-state academic recognition. Dietz brought up the fact that Hedberg had told him, even though Sloan was a good basketball player, he thought he was a better tennis player. "That was pretty shocking to me," Sloan remembered, "because I had started playing tennis a lot later in life and never really had any coaching before I worked with Coach Hedberg, and I felt I had played basketball my whole life. It made me feel good and more confident that Coach Hedberg felt that way about me."

It's funny what athletes remember about their coaches. It's those kind of connections and experiences at critical life moments that draw people together and create life-long relationships and memories. Kids don't forget. Sloan went on to say, "What I remember most of Coach Hedberg is all the laughs and talks we had on our long car rides with Mark and I. Just lots of good times and memories, and I'm glad we had that opportunity that a lot of other kids didn't get. We always knew that Coach had our backs in any situation, and it was cool to know we had the support of someone that was as talented as he was as a player and as a coach. Rural had to feel extremely lucky to pry him away, and I'm sure they knew they were." Rural's AD was elated. I can attest to that.

WHAT WENT INTO HEDBERG'S DECISION TO TEACH/COACH AT WASHBURN RURAL

Hedberg interviewed for our vacancy at Washburn Rural in the spring of 1991. I was the school's athletic director at the time and, based on what I already knew about Kevin Hedberg because of his Seaman days, combined with our Principal Bill Edwards knowing Kevin personally, there appeared to be no negatives associated with this hire. No one had anything but praise for Hedberg at Seaman High. They were not happy about losing such a fine teacher and coach, but they were professional about his choice to move. That did not surprise me in the least.

"I came to Rural because of multiple factors," Hedberg said. "Doug Stanley (a middle school teacher for Rural and a friend of Kevin's) let me know my eighth grade daughter, Tracy, was struggling attitude-wise." So there was the family factor.

Hedberg also knew a couple of Rural girl tennis players. "Danielle Knipp and Kelley Roberts were (tennis) students of mine, and it was tempting to want to coach them." They represented the kind of quality tennis talent Rural had and would have.

Also, a Seaman colleague, Bill Annan, had already been hired by Rural as a business teacher and head girls basketball coach. Hedberg admits, "I had a case of the grass being greener." But make no mistake, helping with his daughter's development was the most important factor in his decision to change schools. I'm certain there was also that curiosity factor wondering what another school community had to offer him.

The table was set for what would be a more than a thirty-year career at Washburn Rural. When I really got a chance to know Kevin—to work alongside him—he quickly became a very respected and admired staff member at Washburn Rural. I would say he soon developed into one of the leaders that the Rural staff looked up to, just like his former colleagues at Seaman.

He became my personal source for local and national political information. His classroom was always near the west office where my office was located, and I would relish times spent talking with Kevin both passing in the hallway and in his classroom. We'd talk about politics, about school issues, about teaching and coaching, but just about anything you could talk about was more enjoyable with a gentleman like Kevin. He became a good friend. To lots of folks at Washburn Rural. As Seaman educator Ron Vinduska said so aptly, "You could trust Kevin." That was fact.

He eventually became our department chair for social studies at Rural. He spent many years teaching Advanced Placement courses and was a well-respected classroom instructor. An exemplary educator.

TWO HEAVY HITTERS AT RURAL KNEW HEDBERG PERSONALLY AND PROFESSIONALLY

Hedberg had graduated from Topeka High School. A couple of Washburn Rural folks—one the acting principal and the other a successful tennis coach in his own rite—certainly helped the cause of hiring Kevin Hedberg at Rural.

The year we hired him, Bill Edwards was the assistant principal at the time, standing in for Principal Bruce Thezan who was serving in Desert Storm. Edwards was also a Topeka High graduate who went to high school at the same time as Hedberg. Bob Gladfelter was also a successful Topeka High grad, and one who had a successful coaching run in tennis at Topeka West. He then became the girls coach at Rural and continued building the groundwork for the tradition in that program. Gladfelter not only knew of Kevin, he had the opportunity to coach against his Seaman teams for eleven years. Bob respected Hedberg as a tennis coach, and he knew he was a great person as well.

I had the opportunity to have lunch with these two former colleagues and friends, and they very willingly gave me their reflections about Kevin.

Edwards remembered that Kevin used to play French horn in the high school instrumental band. He also remembers him being among the group that played some tennis at Hughes tennis courts. Edwards said many of us just played, but Kevin was "really good" and, as a youngster, got sponsored by one of the tennis companies. With that, Hedberg received really nice rackets. Although he could show the rackets to his friends, he couldn't let them play with them or let them have any of the equipment. Sponsor's policy. Hedberg was very cautious about that. "When he walked on the court, he was not just an easy-going, jovial kid, but then he got real serious when he played." Hedberg had that competitive switch that all good athletes have. When it was on, so was his tennis game.

Gladfelter had overheard Hedberg telling high school players to "concentrate on the point." In Hedberg's teaching, each point should be their only focus. Both Edwards and Gladfelter mentioned that we all had worked with coaches who, when they could best relate well with kids in their sport, often seemed to be the most successful in the classroom as well. Hedberg could work with kids in any capacity. He worked as well with the most successful, bright kids as he did with the kids with lesser abilities. Or with the ones that lacked self-motivation. His interest was their development and their experiences. He worked hard to enhance those experiences. Kevin focused on the "we" as in team and not the "I" as the individual. However, he wanted what was best for EACH kid too. Sometimes a tough balancing act.

Edwards remembered a group of college male staff members at Washburn University who used to get together and play tennis. Hedberg's father was in the group. Apparently when they played tennis it got serious. Kevin may have gotten that ability to focus on the tennis courts from his father.

COACH WAS WELL RESPECTED—AS A HUSBAND AND FATHER

While being a father had a bit to do with Hedberg's move to Washburn Rural, it was interesting to find out from his wife, Sherri, what kind of a family man this excellent teacher and coach really was.

When I asked Sherri when she first met Kevin, she mentioned that it was through private tennis lessons. While Kevin was working at Topeka Country Club, Sherri's father thought it might be a good idea for his young daughter and her sister to take tennis lessons. Sherri was twenty-two when she met the tennis instructor. Young Sherri says she was smitten by Hedberg.

"I thought he was the best-looking guy I'd ever seen and wanted to go out with him." And she did. They dated for a while, but then, according to Sherri, life got in the way. The two went their separate ways and both married—someone else.

But ten years later, late in 1984, there was a chance meeting at a local Topeka restaurant called Bennigans. By this time, Hedberg was divorced from his first wife and was enjoying dinner and drinks with Bob Chipman who was coaching basketball at Washburn University. Sherri also was divorced, but didn't know Kevin was single again. She and her friend went over to Hedberg and Chipman's table and struck up a conversation. While that all sounds very storybook, it quickly developed into another dating relationship. In 1985 the couple married. Those of us who believe in fate will have a wonderful time with that chance meeting and eventual developments of romance. You couldn't write a better scenario.

Kevin has a daughter, Tracy, from his first marriage. Eventually, the newlyweds—Kevin and Sherri—had Trevor. Kevin was teaching and coaching at Seaman, and Sherri worked as a court reporter—her career path since she was nineteen. Some of her longer workdays were put in reporting for the Kansas Corporation Commission. She would often find herself working twelve-hour days, so there was the need for Kevin to be flexible even though he was. Kevin has always been a guy to say, "Whatever it takes to get this done."

Both court reporting and teaching/coaching placed real demands on both of their time. Sherri said that when Trevor was preschool age, the couple had good support and help from Kevin's parents. When schedules got really busy, there were times that Kevin took Trevor to tennis meets with him. Sherri would occasionally take Trevor to her office, and Trevor entertained himself on the computer with games and such. Sherri was also able to take Fridays off when Trevor was young, and they would often go do fun things together.

Sherri commented on Kevin's loyalty to his kids. Her step-daughter Tracy spent time at their home, and Kevin helped with every part of Trevor's growing years. According to Sherri, Trevor's favorite sport was originally basketball, and Kevin helped him with that development. Due to some injuries, Trevor picked up tennis, and as he developed more as a player and became older, Kevin put his racket away for awhile to devote his time to help Trevor become a very good tennis player. Trevor was at Washburn Rural when the boys tennis team had its most incredible run of success at the state level.

All in all, Sherri says that she and Kevin have always been very compatible. They enjoy traveling and vacations, and Sherri describes her and Kevin as the "perfect travel companions." She also mentioned that they are both lifelong learners who love to read. Kevin's broad knowledge base made him a very good Trivial Pursuit player. His games of trivia at home were legendary.

While he still loves tennis and enjoys watching it on television, he also likes following NBA basketball and is an avid Chiefs fan. The Chiefs defeating the Philadelphia Eagles in Super Bowl 57 undoubtedly brought joy to the Hedberg home. In 2022, the couple enjoyed thirty-seven years of marriage, and both will be retired in 2023.

FROM TREVOR HEDBERG

Kevin and Sherri's son together, Trevor, is a very learned individual. He has his Doctorate in philosophy. With the PhD, he has worked at multiple colleges in the U.S. and, at the writing of this book, is a professor at the University of Arizona. Trevor is a thinker, so his responses to my questions characterize a good deal of thought and reflection. I had the good fortune of knowing Trevor for his four years of high school at Rural. He was a major contributor to three state team tennis titles in 2003, 2004 and 2005. He was on a state championship doubles team in 2005. As successful as Trevor was on the tennis courts, he was equally gifted in the classrooms. He graduated from college with a 4.0 grade average, and he had many choices when it came to selecting a college to attend and choosing a major to pursue. I thought it would be interesting to find out if and how his parents played a role in his love for learning and academia.

Trevor's reflection: "Both of my parents were generally all-in on whatever ambitions I had. (I doubt they would have supported grossly unethical goals, but mine didn't fit that description.) I was a pretty motivated student, so I didn't need much encouragement to do my schoolwork. Both my parents were actually pretty big on trying to promote a balanced approach to schoolwork—understanding it as only one component of a well-rounded and fulfilling childhood and adolescence. This meant that they were willing to let me stay home from school for illness more often than some other parents and tried to make sure I had ample time for sports and leisure. So I learned from a young age that there was more to life than school. I did ultimately graduate from college with a 4.0 GPA, hold a PhD in philosophy, and am currently a professor at the University of Arizona. So I think we can safely conclude that their parenting choices did not hinder my intellectual development.

"I do remember one particular thing my father helped me with in middle school: the asinine Accelerated Reader program. Instead of having you do a traditional book report, this system had you take a multiple-choice quiz to get the "points" attached to the book, and you had to get a certain number of points each semester. This is a terrible system for encouraging kids to read (because it relies entirely on extrinsic motivation), but that's a topic for another time. Anyway, I failed the very first reading quiz I ever took after reading through a book for eight weeks, and after explaining my distress to my parents, my dad suggested that he and I read some books on the reading list together, and he would help me prepare for the quizzes. It worked, and we read many classic books like *Treasure Island* and *The Call of the Wild* along the way.

"But I'd say my dad's biggest influence was in helping me pursue tennis more seriously during high school. He knew what it took to be successful with tennis and was willing to invest the time on court (in what were essentially free private lessons) to help me improve. But the bigger commitment was all the weekends he gave up to help me travel to tournaments. Without even counting the high school tennis season, it would have amounted to about twenty weekends a year and who knows how much money. And of course, I played on three state championship teams that he coached (2003–2005) and won state doubles in 2005. That's the kind of experience you typically only get once in your life."

It is safe to say that Kevin and Sherri valued a well-rounded individual—one healthy in mind and body. And, just like with the help Kevin gave Trevor with the reading assignments in middle school, Kevin indirectly likely contributed to Trevor's understanding of problem-solving as a parent. Kevin's response was not to run to the school and complain because the reading program was not a motivation for Trevor to read. He problem-solved and found a way he could directly assist Trevor with enjoying reading. After all, according to Sherri and also what I know about Kevin, he too loves to learn.

Trevor has fond memories of his parents when he was a younger kid, but something that sticks out to him as a vivid memory is the time his father became gravely ill. When you are four, you have some recollection, a perspective, and that perspective was one of being frightened and that feeling even little kids can get when something isn't right.

Here's Trevor's recollection of the episode: "By far my strongest early childhood memory of my dad is when he almost died. When he was forty and I was four, he suffered severe pancreatitis due to gall bladder stones that originated from a blood transfusion he had received as a three-year-old. When you have pancreatitis, they run tests of your blood—usually looking at levels of lipase and amylase because elevated levels of those enzymes provide insight into how severe the condition is. I am no medical practitioner, but one of the doctors who tended to my dad during his hospitalization said that his blood counts were a record high for a survivor at Stormont Vail. (Occasionally, when they would run into each other in the future, he would remind my dad that he still held the record.) If the doctors were gamblers, there's no doubt they would have wagered against his survival.

"At such a young age, I didn't really understand the gravity of the situation but still had an intuition that something was wrong. There was an eerie emptiness at home. When he did return—after six weeks in the hospital and with one less gall bladder—things got back to normal. But as I got older, I realized just how loudly the reaper had knocked on his door and wondered how much different my life would have been if things had unfolded differently. Without my dad, I would have almost surely gone to a different high school, and it's doubtful I would have taken up tennis. This would have had a ripple effect regarding who my friends were, where I went to college, and so on. My entire life would have been radically different. And of course, the many thousands of students he had in the three subsequent decades would have never interacted with him."

Having been a survivor of cancer, I understand myself what a profound effect a life-threatening illness can have on your perspective of life. It changes you. No doubt. And I can certainly relate to Trevor's thoughts about how a different outcome for his father could have and would have altered his life path. Much like Kevin's life would have been altered had he chosen a different school to attend after high school, or not returned to Topeka to work at the Topeka Country Club, imagine how devastating it would have been for Trevor to lose his father at age four. Based on the severity of those consequences and, fortunately, a positive outcome, this period of time is permanently etched into Trevor's mind as it likely is in Kevin's.

I was also curious about what it was like to grow up with Kevin Hedberg since he was such an admired instructor and also a successful high school tennis coach. After all, Trevor himself became a college professor, teaching and influencing young minds, and he also took up the sport that his father is so passionate about and spent the better part of fifty-seven years playing and coaching. It would be hard not to be influenced by your father and eventually to recognize how he excelled at his vocation.

Trevor said : "Perhaps surprisingly, I did not come to fully understand this until my twenties. I took much of my dad's expertise and (for lack of a better word) reasonableness for granted when I was younger. On the coaching side, I saw a lot of less-than-stellar college coaching. In some cases, the coach's behavior was grossly unethical (e.g., violating rules on recruiting), and in others, it was just incompetent. In high school, our schedule of events was always planned in ways that allowed adequate time for rest in between, and we always got to where we were playing early. We were never disadvantaged because of issues with travel or rest. Without going into details, I'll just say that was definitely not the case in college.

"In both teaching and coaching, my dad made an effort to understand people's motivations and work within their personal values. Different players needed different types of coaching. For example, some needed strategic advice while others just needed a little guidance on keeping a level head in pressure moments. To the extent he could, he tried to do the same thing in his teaching—getting to know the students' needs and responding accordingly. This sounds simple, but it takes a tremendous amount of effort and empathy to do."

I would echo and second Trevor's thoughts. Kevin was all about making the experience of learning and playing tennis a good one. It didn't matter if you were the best player or the fifteenth best player. He wanted the experience of participating to be worth it and of value to each individual's needs. As will be mentioned later in the book, there were multiple tennis players who forsook a portion of their high school season to pursue scholarship "exposure" through their participation in the Missouri

Valley circuit. When a student would choose to bypass the end of their season, which would have included the regional and state tournament opportunities, it would have been easy for him to look at the decision selfishly. As a coach, you want to have your team excel. He also had to deal with the feelings of other teammates who may not have liked the decision to leave their team to pursue the Missouri Valley circuit. Kevin had to deal with both factors. His disappointment never showed up when talking to either the player who elected to do this or when he addressed it with his team.

As to how Kevin's thoughts and actions influenced Trevor he had this to say: "My father, though he was no scholar of moral philosophy, seemed to adhere to a particular moral principle that I am convinced is responsible for much of his success as a teacher, mentor, and coach. One of the most influential principles in the history of moral philosophy is Immanuel Kant's second formulation of the Categorical Imperative. That's quite a mouthful, but in layman's terms, here's the gist of it: in your actions, strive to treat other people as ends in themselves and never merely as a means to your own ends. At its core, this principle is about respecting other people's rationality and autonomy. When you treat someone unfairly to benefit yourself or lie to them because it would be inconvenient to tell them the truth or coerce them into doing something on your behalf, you treat them like an object rather than treating them like a person—a paradigm case of disrespecting their proper status as a rational, autonomous agent.

"I teach and write about ethics professionally, and I have met many ethicists who study Kant. But my father does the best job of anyone I know at treating others—including those he deeply dislikes—with basic respect and dignity. He always seems to create a memorable and positive impression on others, and I think this is the biggest reason why. This is not just a public practice or façade: he does this in his private life as well. I have particularly admired his unwillingness to engage in petty gossip or bad-mouthing of people behind their back. If he has an issue with someone, he will address the matter with them in a more diplomatic and productive way. In my own dealings with people, I try to model this behavior toward my friends, coworkers, and students. But I recognize I still often fall short of the standard he sets."

When you consider the big picture of how one functions in the world, isn't a respectful demeanor something to strive for and admire about those who live that way daily? Kevin may be one of the individuals who has very few, if any, detractors. He has treated others how he would himself like to be treated. And that, in and of itself, is an impressive accomplishment.

Unbeknownst to Trevor, when I asked if there were some final words or reflections he'd like to share about his father, his words closely mirrored Rick Peterson's foreword from this book. Trevor said: "The world is filled with lots of people who are very successful and accomplished. And if one's profession is noble, it's good to have success in your field. But many achieve that success at the expense of others or by bending moral rules to serve their self-interests. The most important thing to understand about my dad is that he never engaged in these sorts of behaviors. The adage "Nice guys finish last" suggests that people who are virtuous and generally uphold their moral integrity will be tricked, outmaneuvered, or otherwise out-competed by those who are more willing to behave unscrupulously. I have long been skeptical of this outlook, but in my own life, I can think of no better counterexample to it than my dad's career. His success—both in terms of awards received and positive influence on others—was achieved not in spite of his conscientiousness and concern for others but because of it. I hope others will evaluate my life the same way when it is over."

Finally Trevor had this to share about both his parents: "When I reflect back on my behavior when I was younger, I do wish that I had generally shown more gratitude toward my parents. In graduate school, I met lots of aspiring PhDs who had strained relationships with their parents. In many cases, their parents did not support their career aspirations. As I came to understand that the help and support I received was uncommon, I grew to appreciate it more deeply. Whenever I enjoyed some new achievement (e.g., publishing a paper, defending my dissertation, getting into graduate school), one of the first things my dad would tell me was to thank the people who had helped me. I wish I had developed that value at a younger age and expressed my thanks to him a little more often."

How special is it to an individual and special for their parents to say and hear these words. Legacy established by Kevin and Sherri Hedberg.

Kevin Hedberg while playing collegiately at the University of South Florida. Hedberg made the team's top six his freshman year.

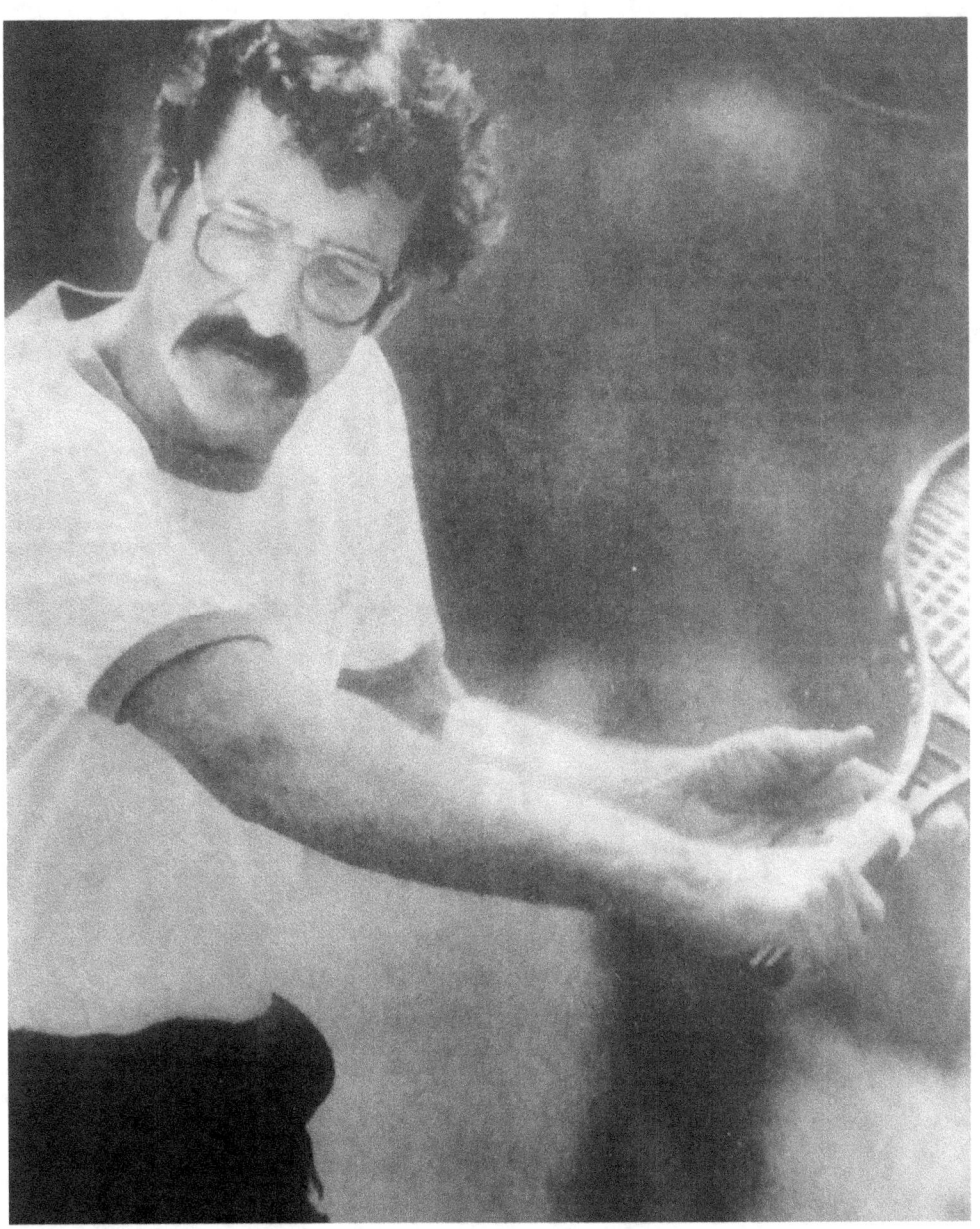

Hedberg for many years played in Topeka's annual Memorial Day tennis tournament. Here he advances to the quarterfinals at the then Winter Park which later became Kossover tennis courts.

Back in 1971 Topeka hosted a July 4th tennis tournament and back in the day The Topeka Capital-Journal covered the local sports scene vigorously. At its peak there were more than a dozen writers devoured to local and area sports. In this Neff Jacobson photo they used the clean cut Hedberg referring to him as, "Ex-Topeka High star."

(Photo credit: *Topeka Capital-Journal*)

Kevin and Sherri's wedding in 1985

(Top) As an adult in this Missouri Valley-sanctioned tournament Hedberg was privileged to play a gentleman he idolized, Van Thompson, nearly a decade older than Hedberg. Hedberg won the match and the tournament over Thompson, then a social studies teacher at Eudora, Kansas

(Bottom) Tracy and Trevor Hedberg

Coaching Legacy of Champions

A couple of Washburn Rural coaching legends. Both Bill Annan and Kevin Hedberg joined the Rural teaching staff in the fall of 1991 after both having taught at Topeka-Seaman

1993- 6A - State Champions

(Top) In 1992 Coach Kevin Hedberg's first varsity six at Washburn Rural. Left to Right: Jeff Chen, Todd Blanton, Joel Janda, Matt Watson, Kirk Stewart, Ryan Kuhn and Coach Hedberg.

(Bottom) Left to Right: Emily Lee, Jenny VanVlack, Colleen Pedley, Danielle Knipp, Kelly Robert's, Megan McBride, Coach Kevin Hedberg, Assistant Jim Dinkel
1993 5A State Champions

Coaching Legacy of Champions

What better to have to commemorate a once in a lifetime event but a screen printed T-shirt.

Kevin Hedberg returning to the campus of South Florida University where he played collegiately.

Along the way Kevin Hedberg garnered much deserved honors as did his players. Here he speaks on behalf of Danielle Knipp at the United States Tennis Association (USTA) at her induction. Finding the right words is one of Hedberg's gifts.

(Top) 2001 Regional at Kosover Tennis Courts. Hedberg gives coaching to Ben Wiechman helping him to a 4th place singles finish.

(Bottom) Hedberg and his 2005 State Champs inducted into Washburn Rural's Hall of Fame. From Left to Right: Coach Hedberg, Zach Newell, Trevor Hedberg, Drew Hanson, Sumeet Patel and Ben Newell. These five players emassed a career total of 13 All State Awards as individuals.

For many of Hedberg's coaching years coaches were not allowed to talk to their players during a match. This changed and Hedberg took full advantage of working with his athletes with in-match strategies.

Hedberg made a decision to leave the world of private lessons for adults to coach high school athletes. There would be numerous photos like this after the elation of completing a high school career at the state tournament.

(Top) 2005 State Champions in their youthful days.
(Bottom) A Washburn Rural tradition established by the Art Department, a mural of an outstanding educators painted near the cafeteria entrance. Kevin Hedberg with his likeness.

Coaching Legacy of Champions

BOYS TENNIS AT WASHBURN RURAL 1980-1990

It's worth noting that, prior to Hedberg's time at Washburn Rural, there was already some excellence in boys tennis. In the spring of 1988, as a team, Rural won its first state championship in 5A. Powell Crosley, who had won a state championship in singles in 1986, again led the 1988 team to a team championship, winning his second state title. Rural also was the Regional champion in 1988.

Washburn Rural dominated the Centennial League in the 1980s. They were league champions eight of the ten years in that decade, 1981-1988.

In 1983 Houston Pulford and Sean Roberts captured the 5A state doubles championship. And in 1984 Jeff Watson and Mark Dillon were third place at the 5A state championships.

The Topeka City championship eluded Rural with the likes of Topeka West and Topeka High to contend with though. With Hedberg at the helm, that would soon change.

During the '80s, Kevin Hedberg became really familiar with the tennis players at Washburn Rural, many of whom he gave private lessons to in the off-season. There was a good pipeline being established at Washburn Rural, and Hedberg, along with the rest of the city, recognized this talent-laden school community.

HEDBERG'S FIRST BOYS SEASON 1992 SAW FIRST CITY CHAMPIONSHIP FOR RURAL

In the year 1992, George H.W. Bush was president. Then in November, Bill Clinton was elected. Baseball player Barry Bonds signed the most lucrative contract to date at $4.7 million with the Pittsburgh Pirates. *The Silence of the Lambs* was tabbed best movie of the year. And Sports Illustrated selected tennis player Arthur Ashe as the Sportsperson of the Year. There's some irony.

That same year, the Kevin Hedberg era began at Washburn Rural High School in Topeka, Kansas. After spending the last eleven years at Seaman High, Hedberg knew Rural's returning players due to play in the spring of his first year. He was confident his two best players at Rural could compete for a Topeka City championship.

Shae Wright and Phillip Pepperdine were supposed to return for the 1990-91 school year, but Hedberg was thrown a curve. Wright transferred to Arkansas City, Kansas, and Pepperdine to Lawrence, Kansas. Now, all bets were off. Incidentally, Wright went on to capture a 5A state tennis title at Ark City. Pepperdine eventually returned to Rural. More on that later.

However, there was a transfer student who landed at Rural. Matt Watson.

Two brothers of Watson—Jeff and Jimmy—had previously played tennis at Rural. In 1983-84, Jeff placed third in doubles with partner Mark Dillon. In 1985, the doubles team of Jimmy Watson and Powell Crosley entered the tournament as the number one seed. So Watson's bloodline was a good one. His family moved back to Topeka which would play out well for Rural tennis.

Washburn Rural had previously won the 1988 5A State title but had not won a City championship to date.

Matt Watson had won three consecutive Wyoming state titles. He came into the Topeka City championship and defeated Hayden's number one singles player, Jamie Conway, 6-2, 6-1. Additionally, Rural's Todd Blanton won the number two singles, defeating Shawnee Heights Jeff Rinker 8-3 for the championship.

In a Topeka Capital-Journal article written by sportswriter Kevin Haskin, Hedberg said, "I thought with those two (Wright and Pepperdine) we'd be a shoo-in to win city. Then we didn't have them, but we got a gift with Watson moving in. And what can you say about Todd Blanton? He's a basketball player who plays tennis in the spring." In other words, a good athletic kid who could be coached in the nuances of tennis.

Both of Rural's double teams added second-place showings. Ryan Kuhn and Jeff Chen were the number one doubles team. Kirk Stewart and Joel Janda played number two doubles. With the 28 team points, Washburn Rural won their FIRST ever Topeka City championship. They outscored second place Topeka West by three points.

Hedberg told Haskin, "I felt like we really competed for the first time this year."

Watson defeated Conway who came into the tournament 10-0. According to the article, it was an exceptionally windy day, and it affected play. According to Haskin, Watson won his match with a combination of spin, touch and power.

Watson said, "It's hard to tell by the score, but Jamie gave me a good match. That first set was tough," he continued. "I thought the score would be closer, but when the big points came up, it seemed like I'd win them." Watson was also content to just keep the ball in play and hope the breeze defused Conway's power.

"The first opportunity I got, I wanted to take advantage of it," Watson said. "I always try to live by the strategy that you only have to hit one winner per point. So, I just waited for my shot, and the wind played a big factor today, so that was important."

In what would be the move-in's ONLY year and Coach Hedberg's first year, Washburn Rural had its first ever city championship. Little did anyone know that Rural would reel off twenty more consecutive years of city championships—a total of twenty-one straight between 1992-2012. After losing one in 2013, they ran off six more years—2014-2019—a total of twenty-seven in twenty-eight years. A pretty remarkable run. Hedberg's timing was good, maybe his guidance and leadership was spot on, but of course, he would credit the fantastic tennis players that Rural continued to churn out year after year.

Later that season, Washburn Rural also captured the Centennial League championship. Watson beat Conway again in number one singles. Blanton finished second in number two singles, beaten by Rooks from Hayden 6-2, 7-6. The number one doubles team of Kuhn and Chen finished second to Riddle and Sloan—the players from Hedberg's former team, Seaman. Washburn Rural won the team championship by four points over Emporia, 21-17.

At Regionals, Watson qualified for state as runner-up to Wichita Southeast's Simon Evelyn 6-4, 6-7 and 7-5. Todd Blanton also qualified for the State tournament despite losing his consolation match to Southeast's Shiloh Booth 6-0, 6-2.

There would be no state placing for Rural as a team, but Watson placed eighth as a singles player. So, the table was set, and the strong tradition was ready to get even stronger.

REFLECTION BY PLAYER MATT WATSON

"We (family) had moved to Cheyenne, Wyoming in January of 1988, and suddenly, we were moving back to Topeka in January of 1992 for my last semester of high school. I was less than thrilled to move with one semester left, but one thing that became a positive of the move was that I was going to get an extra season of high school tennis that spring as boys tennis was in the fall in Wyoming. It also meant playing for the same high school that two of my brothers, Jeff and Jim, played for and had very successful high school careers. My brother Jeff finished third place in 5A doubles, and my brother Jimmy was the #1 seed at state in doubles his senior year.

"Prior to my move, Coach Hedberg had taken over at Washburn Rural, and I was very aware of his coaching talent from my early years of playing tennis in Topeka. I was also very familiar with several of the players that were slated to play on the team that year—Ryan Kuhn (a neighborhood friend for years that I introduced to tennis), Kirk Stewart, Phillip Pepperdine and Shae Wright. We also had a younger player (sophomore I believe) Jeff Chen who was very talented. This team was poised to make a strong run at the state title. I then heard from Coach Hedberg that Phillip and Shae were both moving away and, while the team was going to be strong, we had lost two of our top players. Coach Hedberg met with me to discuss my thoughts of whether I would like to play doubles or singles in order to give myself the best chance at a Kansas state title. In my high school career in Wyoming, I had finished second in doubles my freshman year, won state in doubles my sophomore year and then won back to back singles titles my junior and senior year. I was humbled that he would ask me what I wanted to do versus simply doing what he thought would be best for the team. It has never escaped me that he gave me that opportunity to decide which I would like to do to finish out my high school career.

"As it turned out, I ended up playing #1 singles that season. We had an athlete (not a tennis player) at #2 singles in Todd Blanton. He was your summer tennis player that simply knew how to compete and win matches—much more of an athlete than a tennis player. Todd ended up having a very successful season for us that year and accomplishing a lot more than I think any of us thought he would. Ryan Kuhn and Jeff Chen played #1 doubles and also had a very successful season and qualified for state. I believe Todd lost in the finals of regionals but made it to state. I had a very successful regular season with one loss. We were at a tournament (Salina maybe) and I was up 7-2 or 7-3 and ended up losing 9-7. I recall being extremely frustrated and disappointed that I did not close out the match and taking my first loss on my record. I vividly remember Coach Hedberg talking to me after the match about the positive regarding that loss and how it could serve a couple of positive purposes: First, it would remind to maintain focus until the end and not take ANY lead for granted. Second, he said it would alleviate some pressure for me so that I did not have to listen to others talking about "my undefeated season" and what that pressure might mean later in the season. That conversation certainly helped me recover mentally, and I went on to finish out the regular season unblemished.

"Our first goal that year was to win the city championship which I don't think had ever been done. If it had, it had been a very long time. We had a great weekend, and I recall beating Jamie from Hayden High School in the finals. I remember it being one of the better matches that season and winning fairly convincingly in what was anticipated as a very tough match. Jamie played well that day, but I just had one of those matches where I was very locked in and made very few mistakes. I remember Coach Hedberg and I talking about what those victories would mean for our team (both for me and our other teams playing) and for me in regards to my legacy at Washburn Rural. We were able to win the city championship that year, and it began a streak of Washburn Rural winning city for many years to come. I believe they went on to win every city championship over the next twenty-plus years except for one. It is a fond memory to think back that our team was the start of that success for Coach Hedberg at Rural.

"Coach Hedberg continued to be a mentor and coach for me after my high school career finished. I went on to play varsity tennis at Washburn University, and I vividly remember calling him at one point during my freshman year as I was struggling some during my first year of tennis. I had been accustomed to a lot of success on the court and, suddenly, I was struggling to win matches. We would visit about the challenges of adjusting to college life and how that affected my play, the adjustments to college tennis and the elevated level of toughness it took to compete against all very high level players. At one point, I remember going out to Washburn Rural a couple of times, and he would hit balls with me and offer advice on how I could develop my game further to best contend at the collegiate level. He encouraged me to play as many tournaments as I could that summer after my freshman year and specifically to work on attacking my backhand more. I committed to his advice and took quite a few lumps at the start of the summer to guys I knew I could have beaten playing my prior style, but by the time my sophomore season was underway, I was suddenly beating conference players handily that I struggled with the prior year. He was instrumental in getting me to the next level as I would then go on to have very successful junior and senior years, especially, accumulating twenty-plus wins in both singles and doubles in those campaigns. I know that would not have been possible without his continued guidance and insight.

"When I think about the most influential coaches I've had throughout my tennis career, it really narrows down to two—Larry Haughness…who was my pro in Cheyenne the four years I was there…and Coach Hedberg. Certainly, I've had many coaches who have helped shape and develop my game, but those two had the most lasting impact on me to this day. His (Hedberg's) character, support, leadership and insight were incredible building blocks for me, and I will always be grateful for his guidance those 4.5 years at Washburn Rural and then Washburn University. It is especially impressive considering we were together one semester at Washburn

Rural. I know I was just one player of many that holds Coach Hedberg in high regard, and it speaks volumes to his legacy as a tennis coach and as a person."

Matt Watson—Washburn Rural High School Class of 1992

1993—YEAR TWO FOR BOYS

In the early years of the Hedberg-coached era at Rural, the boys tennis team set the standard for playing well, especially in the city school competition and in the Centennial League meet. After the season, Hedberg told the school's yearbook reporter that, "This team proved itself in the best meets. We are starting a tradition of rising to the moment." That commentary proved quite prophetic and became the reality for Washburn Rural tennis the next thirty years.

With only two of the previous year's top six returning—Ryan Kuhn, a junior, and Kirk Stewart, now a sophomore—it was a year for newcomers to step up their games. Also, as good fortune would have it, Phil Pepperdine returned to Washburn Rural after a year's absence.

At the tough Topeka City meet, Kuhn and Stewart teamed up to win the number one doubles event. Pepperdine finished second in the number one singles event. Juniors Matt Barreto and Ryan Laughon also took second in the number two doubles event. And newcomer and freshman Brian Hejtmanek won the number two singles event. The team played well enough to win the city team championship.

At the Centennial League tournament, Kuhn and Stewart again set the pace with a win in number one doubles. Pepperdine and Hejtmanek finished first place in their number one and number two singles events. Barreto and Laughon completed the sweep of first place winners by capturing the number two doubles event.

Kuhn and Pepperdine combined to win the doubles championship at regionals and qualified for the state tournament.

Hejtmanek described well what it was starting to mean to make the top six at

Rural. "I'm glad I got the chance to play varsity as a freshman," Hejtmanek said. "I learned a lot from the upperclassmen on the team. They taught me everything I know." Hejtmanek and Pepperdine went 17-4 and 17-3 respectively playing a lot of the singles events in '93. Kuhn went 18-2, Laughon 16-8, Barreto 13-7 and Stewart 14-6.

This team had a great chemistry and a keen sense of camaraderie and, with the help of humor, they became a close-knit group. Laughon told the yearbook that, "The funniest part of the season had to be the mystery behind Hedberg's clipboard at Junction City." This team was not above pranking their esteemed coach, and they were inclined to poke fun at each other.

Most importantly in Hedberg's first two years at Rural, he was able to continue to build upon the pride and tradition of Washburn Rural's men's tennis program. Success breeds success. And combine talent with coaching, it can be really good.

1994—FAMILIAR FACES RETURN TO THE COURTS

Beginning Hedberg's third season as boys coach, Hedberg knew the sophomores who were there for his first two previous seasons. They were now his senior leaders. The longer you coach kids, the more they know your expectations.

The previous year, the boys captured both the city and the league championships. The two league championship wins extended Rural's championship streak to four straight years. 1992 and 1993 were the FIRST city championships for Rural. And that group finished eighth at the state tournament. There were also eight returning lettermen coming back for the 1994 season. The prospects looked bright.

Sophomore Brian Hejtmanek, who was 17-6 as a freshman while competing as the number one singles player, was back for season two. Senior Ryan Kuhn was half of the doubles combination who placed third at state with Phillip Pepperdine. Kuhn's other partner from the previous year, junior Kirk Stewart, was part of the team that captured the city and league doubles title.

Three other seniors were competing for playing time. Matt Baretto, Ryan Laughon and Pat Angel would compete with returning junior Todd Abplanalp and sophomore Todd Thelen.

Newcomers to the program were juniors Mike Schwart and freshman Mark McAllister. Both of them would be aiming for top six. Competition breeds a good work environment. Everyone was fighting and clawing, hoping to be in the top six.

In an article for the Capital-Journal's preseason peek by sportswriter Kevin Haskin, Hedberg said, "It's a good bunch. It might well turn out to be the best team I've had since being here. Actually, my top ten or twelve kids are all good players. It's a deal where I'm trying to keep my second six happy so that, when they're a junior or senior, they can help us on the varsity, which is good, but it's a different kind of problem, and I'm not used to dealing with that." Rural had depth in 1994, and that can be both a blessing and a curse depending on how the coach and players handle it.

By the time the city tournament rolled around, Washburn Rural's lineup was set. On an exceptionally windy day, Hejtmanek captured the number one singles championship bringing his record to 11-0. Newcomer McAllister was good enough to capture the city second singles championship. Kuhn and Stewart placed second in number one doubles, falling to Hayden's Dunn and Rooks. But Baretto and Laughon captured the second doubles team championship. Washburn Rural outscored Hayden 30-21 to run their string of city titles to three in a row.

Rural also captured their fifth straight Centennial League title and their fourteenth out of fifteen years. Bareto and Laughon qualified for state. Hejtmanek took fourth at state and McAllister was sixth. At the end of the season, McAllister moved with his family to Chicago leaving that second singles slot open for 1995. Incidentally, McAllister was the Illinois state singles champion in 1995.

1995—STILL BEST IN TOPEKA CITY EVENT

Although 1995 would see their string of Centennial League championships interrupted, Rural dominated the city championship with a 32-22 team victory over second place Topeka West. Brian Hejtmanek and Kirk Stewart both captured singles championships in the number one and number two singles competition.

The Junior Blues also swept the number one and number two doubles titles. David Almeling and Joey Stewart won the number one doubles defeating a Topeka High team 8-5. The number two doubles team of Todd Thelen and Todd Abplanalp also captured the number two doubles event title completing the four-match sweep by Rural.

After the fourth straight Hedberg-led city title, he said in an article by Capital-Journal sportswriter Rick Peterson, "I can smile now. I'm surprised. I really am. Coming in, I was concerned really truthfully about tying it or being able to win it outright. I've seen the Topeka West kids play very well and give us fits, and I was very concerned."

Hedberg reflected on this fourth straight city title at Rural, "This is the first of the four that I'm going to walk away at the end of the day and think, wow, we really couldn't have done any more than we did. The first year (we won) we weren't the best team, flat out. We were very fortunate to just have played well."

This was also the year that the Rural's reign as Centennial League champions ended. The Junior Blues had won five previous league championships. Emporia ended that run. But Emporia had to win all three final matches that they were in to win the team championship. The margin of victory was just three points.

Hedberg, the consummate gentleman, gave Emporia credit, saying, "We had a window of opportunity, but they came through when they had to. My hats off to them." When someone outplays you or are better on a given day, give them their due.

This was not a year that Rural would see post-season wins. Unfortunately. They sent Kirk Stewart, Almeling, Joey Stewart and Hejtmanek to state, but none finished top six.

1996—RETURN TO THE POST SEASON

Washburn Rural tennis teams are used to having success. Although they did not win the Centennial League title in '95, they did capture the Topeka City championship for the fourth consecutive year—991-1995—which just happened to coincide with Hedberg's first four boys seasons he coached at Rural.

In '96, Rural happily received city transfer Danny Williams. Williams was a quality singles player capturing the number two singles event at the city meet. Brian Hejtmanek added the number one singles championship for Rural. Rural did not win their Regional team title, but qualified five out of the six players for 6A state tournament. The Activities Association also designated the Junior Blues as the host for the state tournament.

Brian Hejtmanek qualified for state in the number one singles bracket with a fourth place finish. He had to bow out- default the 3rd place match- due to his back injury. Danny Williams qualified in singles as well. Both doubles teams of Wes Geier and Mike Alva along with David Almeling and Vince Lei qualified for state.

As a team, Washburn Rural finished second place at regionals behind Lawrence which pleased Coach Hedberg.

"We showed up and played real well," Hedberg commented in an article written by Capital-Journal sportswriter Rick Peterson. "We get to host the state tournament and see our kids play and, if we show up and play, regardless of the placement, we'll be okay."

Lawrence captured the regional title. Shawnee Mission East won the state title. At state, after defaulting a couple of matches with the back injury, Hejtmanek still managed to finish sixth in singles. Williams took fifth place at state in singles. Geier and Alva won 8th in doubles while teammates Almeling and Lei took 9th. The team won 3rd place at State that year.

1997—A YOUTH MOVEMENT FOR WASHBURN RURAL

The 1997 spring season of tennis looked to be a rebuilding year. Rural suffered heavy losses to graduation. They lost good senior players from the previous season, so Hedberg told the Capital-Journal it was unlikely that the current team would be as strong as 1996's team. Always good to downplay it for the media.

Sophomore Justin Keller looked to be the number one singles player in the season's preview article. Newcomer David Stauffer, just a freshman, appeared to be the likely number two singles player. That's a young pair to hold down the singles competitions.

Two seniors—who as juniors finished eighth at the state tournament in the number two doubles slot—Wes Geier and Mike Alva, were moving up to the number one doubles slot. As a duo in '96, they had a 26-10 record.

It appeared that juniors David Almeling and Vincent Lei would hold the number two doubles team slot for the 1997 season.

Hedberg's optimism and a little hint of confidence shone through in this preseason preview. Hedberg quietly mentioned, "By May, we could be very good."

Washburn Rural won an early quadrangular that included Topeka High and Topeka West as well as Manhattan. Keller and Stauffer won their singles competitions. Geier and Alva finished second to a good Topeka West doubles team.

Almeling and Lei won the number two doubles. Capturing three out of four events was a good confidence builder for a young team.

In another mid-April quad that included St. Thomas Aquinas, Emporia and Ottawa, the Junior Blues managed a 10-10 tie with Aquinas. Keller took second to an Aquinas player, Stauffer took first over his Aquinas opponent. Alva and Geier took second to an Aquinas duo and Almeling and Lei defeated their Aquinas opponent. Aquinas traditionally fielded a good solid tennis team every year, so it was a positive step for Rural to beat them. Hedberg knew the value of scheduling good competition. It can make you better.

In late April, Washburn Rural won an eight-team event outscoring local city rival Topeka West by eight points, 49-41. Topeka High placed third. Keller and Stauffer both won their singles matches and, in an unusual third singles slot, newcomer McCall also won that singles event. Almeling and Lei took first in the number two doubles to round out a good day on the courts for the young Junior Blue squad.

As predicted in early May, the Junior Blues captured their sixth straight City championship. By Topeka standards, the young Washburn Rural tennis players measured up pretty good. In fact Rural swept all four divisions to defeat runner-up Topeka High 32-23.

"That (string of city championships) isn't something we talk about at school," Hedberg commented, "but I think the boys take a lot of pride in it. I hope they do, because I do." After losing three key players off the previous year's squad, this dominance of city was a pretty significant step for the 1997 team.

"We played really well today, and this team has played well all year," Hedberg added. "I think people thought we would make a real drop, and some kids have really stepped up." Isn't that what sustaining a winning tradition is all about? Good kids do their part, move on, and it's next person up.

Lost to graduation was Brian Hejtmanek, Danny Williams and Todd Thelan.

Keller defeated a very good singles player—Jon Suddarth from Hayden, a junior whose finish marked his third straight year as city runner-up. "If they played tomorrow, it might be a different match," Hedberg cautioned. One thing Keller did very well, according to Hedberg, was handle the big serves from Suddarth.

On May 14, the Junior Blues continued their pursuit of being a "good team" capturing the Centennial League title with a nine-point margin over second place Hayden, 28-17. Keller once again defeated Suddarth in number one singles, 8-5. Stauffer defeated Hayden's DeSilva, 8-2, for the number two singles championship. The doubles teams capped the sweep of first place finishes as Alva and Geier defeated the Shawnee Heights team of Stucky and Barnett 8-6, and Almeling and Lei defeated Hayden's duo of Porubsky and Ragsdale 8-3.

The Capital-Journal article by Rick Peterson went on to quote Hedberg, saying, "It's what you hope for. We knew we had Mike (Alva) and Wes (Geier) coming back, but you bring a freshman in (Stauffer) and he's undefeated at this point. That's pretty incredible."

The storied season took one additional step, but not without some difficulty. During the league tennis meet the week before, Justin Keller had fallen and cracked a bone in his hand and was not available for the regional meet in Leavenworth.

With Keller's 19-1 record on the shelf, number two singles player and freshman David Stauffer stepped up and defeated Topeka High's number one singles player Mike Bonebrake for the regional championship. Geier and Alva beat their teammates of Almeling and Lei for the doubles championship. So Rural captured first and second place in doubles and outdistanced city rival Topeka High 15-9 to advance to state.

Stauffer had played some number one singles and was 8-1 during the season, but credited playing against his teammate Keller in practices all year for his improvement. "Justin and I have been battling all season," he said in Kurt Caywood's Capital-Journal article. "We've worked each other out hard." You get better when you play good competition. Even if it's your own teammate.

1998—EXPERIENCE RETURNING LOOKS TO ENSURE SUCCESS

In the Capital-Journal's preview of city tennis teams, there was a different flavor than '97 for the boys returning for the tennis team. Justin Keller was 19-1 despite having to miss regionals and likely the state tournament as a result of his broken hand. He would be looking for redemption this season.

David Stauffer, as a freshman, made a good showing at state in Keller's absence, finishing seventh at the state tournament in '97. Stauffer, now a sophomore, would be joined by Vincent Lei and David Almeling who finished seventh in doubles the previous year. Gone were state double placers Geier and Alva, but a good crop of underclassmen were prepared to step up and perform well for the Junior Blues. After all, it was their turn.

Hedberg acknowledged that Topeka West should be really good in the city, but also laid out some early expectations saying, "I expect us to have a good team with a chance of placing in the top three at the 6A state tournament." Sometimes you set the bar high and challenge your squad.

Washburn Rural won their quad over Topeka West, sweeping all four divisions.

Keller won the number one singles, and Stauffer won the number two singles. Lei and Almeling won the number one doubles, and the new doubles team of the younger Keller, Jared, and his partner, Blake Asbury, won the number two doubles.

In an early large field tournament at Leavenworth, Washburn Rural finished tied for second with Topeka High as Topeka West beat a strong field by twelve points, 50-38. In the three singles matches, Stauffer finished second to Zovic from Topeka West. Keller won the number two singles match, and newcomer Blake Asbury finished second to Topeka West's VonFelt in the number three singles.

The Junior Blues won the Topeka City team title despite Keller losing to a foreign exchange student from Slovaka, Martin Zlovic, of Topeka West in a 9-7 match. The Junior Blues swept the other three divisions. Stauffer won the number two singles. Almeling and Lei won number one doubles, and Keller and Asbury won number two doubles on the way to the seventh straight city championship for Washburn Rural.

At city, Rural finished with 26 points to Topeka West's 20. "The kids played well. They responded," according to Hedberg's comments in the Capital-Journal article by Pam Clark. Hedberg also said, "I want them to point to this meet and play well. They (Rural) hadn't won one til' they won it seven years ago. I think they take pride in it."

Hedberg was quick to compliment his team's winners. "We had freshmen at number two doubles, and they played like old veterans today. Stauffer is a terrific tennis player, he could play number one singles anywhere. And our two seniors, Almeling and Lei, are National Honors Society members who get the most out of their ability."

Despite Justin Keller's loss at number one singles, Hedberg also said that match was one of the best he's seen. "It was a high level of tennis," Hedberg said, "Make a drop in your mental game, and it's over. I'm not saying that's what happened to Justin, but that match (with Zovic) took a lot mentally. I was very pleased with Justin."

At the Centennial League meet, Washburn Rural took first place in all four events and captured their sixteenth league title in eighteen years. The Junior Blues finished with twenty-eight team points and second-place Shawnee Heights scored seventeen. Keller defeated Suddarth from Hayden for the second straight year.

Keller may have avoided a second injury that year, falling again, but he didn't put his hand down this time.

Washburn Rural did not set themselves up well in the regionals, and their tough draws at the state tournament cost them their shot at being in the top three team finishers. Rural did finish seventh as they came through the consolation matches to finish top ten at state.

1999—CLOSING THE DOOR ON THE '90S; SIX PLAYERS PLACE 6TH OR BETTER AT STATE

Hedberg's decade of the '90s was preparing for its last season before moving into the 21st century. By all indications, the tennis team would just continue its competitive ways and likely just march on and not allow graduation to cause any attrition for their team at all.

A city, league, and regional championship would be earned again. The city championship had been Rural's between 1992-1999—an eight-year string. The Centennial League was Rural's between the years of 1990-1999. No other school won the league in the decade of the 90's. And the boys had captured the regional championships in 1996, 1997, and again in 1999.

David Stauffer would place fourth at the 6A state championship in singles.

In the regionals, Rural and Wichita East both scored thirteen team points, but Rural won the team title based on a tie breaker. Rural qualified all six of its players. East qualified five players. Wichita Southeast did win both the singles and doubles championships.

East's George Hinkle defeated Stauffer in the championship singles match 6-3, 6-0. In doubles, the East duo defeated Rural's Blake Asbury and Jared Keller 6-1, 6-3.

The doubles team of Shane McCall and Matt Larson got a critical third-place finish in number two doubles. Justin Keller also finished fourth place in number two singles, but had to withdraw from the third-place match to Emporia.

On Friday at the state tournament, David Stauffer won his matches, setting himself up for a semifinal match with a victory placing him in the state championship. He would have to defeat Shawnee Mission East's Josh Kopmeyer, who Stauffer defeated earlier in the season.

The other Junior Blue qualifiers survived their first-round matches, but were defeated in round two. Justin Keller also placed 5th in singles.

On Saturday Stauffer took the opening set from the previous year's state champion, Kopmeyer, but fell in the other two sets as Kopmeyer advanced and Stauffer was sent to the third-place match. He finished fourth place, and Asbury and Keller finished fifth place in doubles, and McCall and Larsen finished sixth, which helped Rural to a second-place team finish. Finishing with a state trophy was a highlight for this team.

HEDBERG REFLECTS ON HIS FIRST DECADE—THE '90S

Hedberg said the boys of the 1990-99 period were very memorable. Of course you always remember your first team, and they were very talented and eager. A trend was beginning in the boy's program. Players were starting to elect to attend college AND play tennis. Justin Keller went to Austin-Peay in Tennessee, David Stauffer played at the University of Kansas as did Danny Williams. Matt Watson, who returned from Wyoming for his final season, stayed in Topeka and played at Washburn University.

Another trend that began to develop was, with the excellence of the top players, it was harder and more difficult to make the varsity, top six. Two boys came to Hedberg's mind that set that early example of "those who had to stand and wait." Waiting for their opportunity. Matt Larsen and Shane McCall did so in the 90's. McCall had moved from Sedalia, Missouri where he would likely have been their number two player as a freshman. McCall and Larsen played in a few varsity meets as sophomores and juniors, but mainly played in junior varsity events. Their senior year, they played mostly number-two doubles and some number-one doubles. They helped the team take second place at the state tournament with their sixth-place finish. They lost to Keller and Asbury 9-8—the number one doubles team for Rural that season. "At various points in their high school tennis careers they could have given up and done other things, but they stuck it out and helped make our season so successful," Hedberg reminisced.

2000 BOYS—HOPING FOR ANOTHER GOOD DECADE OF EXCELLENT TENNIS

George W. Bush Jr. won the presidential election by the narrowest of margins over Al Gore. The average cost of a home was $134,000. Gas cost $1.26 a gallon. *Harry Potter and the Goblet of Fire* was published. Tiger Woods became the youngest golfer to win the grand slam of golf. The St. Louis Rams won the Super Bowl 23-16 over Tennessee. Michigan State defeated Florida 89-76 to win the NCAA Basketball Championship.

Truth be known, Kevin Hedberg would take every year one at a time without thoughts about how his teams would do in a ten-year period. He had confidence. Or as he spoke about his demeanor as a tennis player, he could be a bit cocky. Hedberg's current demeanor as a coach never tipped his hand. He kept his confidence to himself. His humility was always first and foremost as to what you observed. And he gave all the credit for success in the program to his tennis players. Always.

Singles stalwart David Stauffer helped lead Washburn Rural to a city, league, and regional championship. The Centennial League championship was Rural's eighteenth in twenty years. That's a lot of wins and only a couple of lesser finishes.

Stauffer again qualified for the state tournament. It was his fourth tournament in his four-year high school career, and it would prove to be his best finish. His efforts helped pave the way for a third-place team finish for the Junior Blues at the Lawrence Tennis Center.

In the semifinal match, Stauffer fell to the eventual 2000 state champion Reckewey from Shawnee Mission South by scores of 6-3, 7-5. After that loss, Stauffer bounced back to defeat Olathe South's Coleman 6-3, 6-0 for an individual third place and helped contribute to a third place team trophy for Rural.

Hedberg told Capital-Journal reporter Rick Peterson, "He got us third place and a trophy, and fourth place gets nothing, so I'm happy with that. I'm sorry to see him go. He's won four league championships, four city championships and been to state four times in singles and won almost one hundred matches. That's not a bad career."

Stauffer, who finished with a 23-4 record, committed to attend Kansas University and play tennis for the Jayhawks.

The Junior Blues got a sixth-place finish from the doubles team of Blake Asbury and Jared Keller but, unfortunately, had to default the fifth-place match because of a nagging, recurring elbow injury for Keller. Hedberg said, "He has a bad case of tennis elbow. I asked him if it hurt to swing the racket, and he said it hurt him to touch the racket, so we decided to play it safe." Hedberg always had his players best interests in mind, especially when it came to their health and welfare. Rural ended the season four points shy of second-place Wichita Southeast and twelve points from the champions, Shawnee Mission South.

At the time, it tied the third best state finish for a Rural boys' tennis team. They had also finished third in 1996.

2001—BEGINNING A DECADE OF DOMINANCE

This tennis season the boys set out to keep their string of city tennis titles going. They had recorded nine straight years of city title wins making them the best local tennis program for a very long time. Could they run their string to ten years?

Indeed. During the course of any tennis season and the off-season, the city's tennis players get along quite well. They play each other often, but when the city bragging rights are on the line, it gets turned up a notch. The year 2001 was no different.

In Rick Peterson's late April article, he asked Hedberg about the fierceness of the city competition among the six high schools. "We like all of those guys," Hedberg stated, "but this is one meet where you show up and try to kill each other." Figuratively speaking, that is, but it only lasts for one meet. Hedberg reminded, "Then, when it's over, you're all friends again, and you go on with your lives." That sounded like a younger Hedberg over at Hughes tennis courts.

Although there were no fatalities recorded, Washburn Rural did enough on the courts during the city event to capture twenty-eight points. The next closest city competitor was Topeka High with twenty-one.

Washburn Rural's two doubles entries captured championships. The number one doubles team of Matt Koupal and Jeff Milberger bested Topeka High's Stanfield and Holdren 8-1, while the other Rural doubles team of Jared Keller and Blake

Asbury defeated High's Wisman and Dunivan almost as easily, 8-3.

Earlier in the year, Keller was playing number-one doubles, but had a playground basketball injury that left him sporting a cast from his hand to his elbow. Hedberg, Keller and his playing partners will forever be indebted to Dr. Pete Lepse who had a son who was a tennis player for Rural. Lepse knew what was needed to keep Keller on the court and effective.

Hedberg had this to say about his powerful doubles teams. "Both of our doubles teams just played beautiful matches." Hedberg went on to say, "They just played very, very well. I think that all the kids showed up ready to play in this meet."

Both Rural's singles teams finished second respectfully. In number one singles, the undefeated Shawnee Heights player, Kinder, defeated Ben Wiechman, 8-3. Topeka High's Rose won the second singles championship, defeating Rural's Fabian Kaelin, 8-4. Kaelin was a foreign exchange student, and one of the few to crack the top six for Washburn Rural.

Hedberg reflected on the tenth straight city championship saying, "You want to play well in this meet because all of these kids know each other." And play well Rural did.

When the Centennial League meet rolled around, at that time, the only non-city team added to the meet was Emporia. But Topeka High and Topeka West were not league schools then, so coaches wanted to continue their dominance in league as well. Washburn Rural did just that, sweeping all four events—number one and two singles and number one and two doubles.

Again, Rural's Wiechman met Shawnee Heights' Kinder, but the outcome was Wiechman 8-1 for a little revenge from the city match. In number two singles, Rural's Kaelin defeated Highland Park's Wassinger for the championship.

The biggest win of the day was Wiechman's win over Kinder. Hedberg had this to say about that victory. "Ben played real well, but Tyler (Kinder) didn't play as well as he's been playing."

Wiechman told Capital-Journal sportswriter Rick Peterson, " It was pretty bad at city. My strokes were going well today, and I was really mentally focused. Last time I don't think I was quite all there as far as my head, but this time I was really focused on the match."

Hedberg told Peterson, "It's been a good day for us," regarding his team's performance. "We came in knowing that we should be pretty safe to win the title if we just played well. And now we are looking at regionals because that's really where it all leads to." Hedberg hoped that the competitive edge his team had built would carry them through regionals for a strong team performance.

With that good performance day—one of many over the previous two decades—Washburn Rural won its twentieth Centennial League title out of the previous twenty-two years. That's being pretty good for a pretty long time.

The next step was regional tennis at Kossover Courts in Topeka. Jared Keller and Blake Asbury not only were tennis partners in doubles, but good friends. Asbury was taken aback when, earlier in the season, Keller broke his wrist playing basketball. But things worked out in the end as the good-friend duo won doubles at regionals and advanced to the state tournament. Asbury and Keller moved their record to 12-0, defeating a Wichita Southeast duo 6-2, 7-5.

Keller won despite being in a cast. His doctor had constructed the cast on his left hand so that he could still toss the ball up for his serve. Initially, Keller told Capital-Journal reporter Rick Peterson, "He (Asbury) was pretty mad at me when it happened. He yelled at me a little bit, but I told him that I was going to play no matter what." Keller thought the cast may have been a blessing and improved his play. He had to concentrate harder on his serves, and Hedberg convinced him to slice his backhand as well.

Asbury and Keller went into the regional seeded number one. "Everybody's kind of out to get you when you're the number one seed, but we played well," Asbury told Peterson. "I kind of lost my head there a few times in that last match, but Jared helped me pull it out."

Asbury and Keller's victory, combined with the other doubles team Jeff Millberger and Matt Koupal placing, vaulted Washburn Rural to the regional championship, holding off second-place Manhattan with a score of 10-9. Millberger and Koupal defeated a Manhattan duo 6-2, 7-5 for third place—same set scores as their teammates Asbury and Keller.

At the state tournament, Asbury and Keller took an even bigger step and captured the state championship in doubles. The Capital-Journal article lead paragraph said,

"Four years of friendship. Four years of hard work. Four years of believing in each other." Both boys had to pass on individual success by not playing singles. "I left it up to them," Hedberg said of their commitment to doubles. "It was their friendship (that kept them together). Singles was just something they couldn't break away and do. We thought they had a chance at this (winning doubles at state), but we also knew either one of them might have a chance at a top-four finish in singles."

There were some anxious moments in the championship when Keller was serving and they fell behind Love-40. They rallied to hold serve and then cruised through the rest of the first set. They trailed 4-3 in the second set but also sandwiched a service break between two service holds for a 6-4 finishing set. They became only the second state doubles champions representing Washburn Rural—joining Sean Roberts and Huston Pulford—who won doubles in the 1983 state championship. Nearly twenty years separated the two great accomplishments. Asbury and Keller ended the season undefeated with a 21-0 record. Cast wrist, but unblemished record in 2001.

With Asbury and Keller's championship, combined with Koupal and Millberger finishing ninth in doubles, the 2001 team finished tied for second place at the state tournament. After the tournament, Hedberg said, "I couldn't be more proud of them (doubles teams). They played really hard and gave a great account of themselves." Rural's state finishes to this point in time were 1st-1988, 3rd-1996, 2nd-1999, 3rd-2000 and 2nd in 2001—four top three finishes at state in six years. Bringing home the hardware.

2002—STARTING TO BE CONSISTENT EXCELLENCE

It was a clean, three-way sweep for the boys tennis team in the spring. They captured the city championship, the league title, and the regional title.

It was the team's eleventh straight city team title which, coincidentally, aligned with Hedberg's eleventh year coaching the boys. It also was the nineteenth Centennial League title in twenty-one years. It was their fourth straight regional title.

Winning the Centennial League title did not come easy. Rural managed to eke out a one-point team victory over Shawnee Heights.

It helped that the doubles team swept championships. Senior Matt Koupal and junior Jeff Millberger won the number one doubles crown with an 8-3 win over an Emporia duo. Freshman Sumeet Patel and John Dageford defeated a Hayden pair for the number two doubles championship, beating them 8-0.

The Shawnee Heights singles players Kinder and Joost swept the singles championships. Both Rural singles players Wiechman and Hanson finished third.

Hedberg offered this tidbit about the league's parity in 2002. "It wouldn't surprise me if we didn't have three state championship trophies coming out of our city this year," referring to Rural (6A), Heights (5A) and Hayden (4A).

At regionals Washburn Rural ended up qualifying five of their six players for the state tournament and won the regional title by a 12-7 margin over Lawrence.

In answer to Capital-Journal sportswriter Chris Wristen's question about dominance, Hedberg replied, "I don't know how dominating we were, but it's nice to win. Today our depth really showed up, and we showed how deep we are as a team."

Ben Wiechman finished second in singles to qualify for state. Sumeet Patel and Drew Hanson won the doubles championship, and the second doubles team of Matt Koupal and Jeff Millberger took third place.

Wiechman missed qualifying for state the year before and was glad to redeem himself. Wiechman said, "I was just glad to qualify after not doing as well at the regional last year, and it was just a bonus to make it to the finals this year and play well."

The freshmen doubles pair of Patel and Hanson expected to contend but would face their city nemeses from Topeka High. The reporter commented that, "Their powerful, driving backhands down the line and whacking aces resulted in a 6-1, 6-3 win." For Patel and Hanson.

Hanson credited their strong beginning 6-1 win with setting the tone. They would take a 20-1 record to the state tournament for pairings.

The Junior Blues finished third place as a team at the 2002 state tournament as the doubles teams scored twenty-two team points, and Wiechman captured five team points with his play in singles. The doubles team of Patel and Hanson finished second, dropping a 7-5, 6-3 match to a Shawnee Mission East team, while Koupal and Millberger claimed a fifth-place state finish.

2003—SECOND STATE TENNIS TITLE FOR THE SCHOOL

The theme of the spring boys' tennis season probably should have contained the word "deep" in it. The Junior Blues had fourteen competent high school tennis players. Enough parity, in fact, that Coach Hedberg entered what typically is referred to as the junior varsity group into several varsity events for the challenge and the more difficult competition.

In an early-season article by Capital-Journal sportswriter Rick Peterson, Hedberg described the depth this way, "I'm not saying that I could take my second team and we could beat anybody, because that's certainly not true, but my kids are very competitive and would do very well in a lot of meets, one through fourteen, right now."

Hedberg defended the split-squad this way, "I think the big thing about tennis is that it's a lifetime sport, and kids just want to play the game. So far they've been willing to tolerate me making decisions about when they play."

The results in the early going supported his decisions. Rural won five of its first six meets entered. They were led by number-one singles player Ben Wiechman and two very good doubles teams consisting of Robbie Simmons and Richard Lin, and Wiles Bobo and Ben Lepse.

It was their twelfth straight city championship beginning in the year 1992. They did it by winning three of the four events. Branden Joost of Shawnee Heights captured the number one singles event. Jeff Millberger and Sumeet Patel won the number one doubles event. Joining them as city champions was the winner of the second singles division, Drew Hanson. Trevor Hedberg (yes, that's Kevin's son, Trevor) and Matt Hansen won the number two doubles event providing a 29-20 team margin over second-place Topeka High.

Hedberg had a pragmatic way of looking at the twelve-year winning streak that happened to coincide with the number of years he had coached at Rural. Hedberg said, "I think a lot of people's perception is that we've just had a lot of good players. I've had my share of really good players in the twelve years, but it's a real tribute to the kids because you have bad days sometimes. They've tended to not have their bad days here, (city event) and that makes it real enjoyable."

While the league may have had a couple of really good individual players that didn't attend Washburn Rural, Rural's depth again showed up. They captured three of the four events at the Centennial League meet, capturing their eighth championship in eight years. And sophomore Drew Hanson staked his claim on the second singles championship, beating Hamilton from Hayden 8-1. Ben Wiechman battled the league's best player, Joost from Shawnee Heights, to capture a second-place finish in number one singles.

The doubles teams of Millberger and Patel and Hedberg and Hanson captured the number one and number two doubles events respectively.

"The kids played real well," Hedberg said. The meet was played on the Washburn Rural home courts. "I think we have an advantage playing here. It's our place, and it's windy, and it's ugly, and I think we play better here." Enough better that they outscored the second place Hayden team 26-18.

At a rainy regional tournament that had to be delayed, Rural netted a perfect score by placing both singles players first and second. The same in the doubles event. Washburn Rural finished one and two in doubles as well.

To notch the perfect eighteen points at regionals, Drew Hanson beat his Rural teammate Ben Wiechman. The doubles team of Millberger and Patel beat their Rural teammates Hedberg and Matt Hansen. Hedberg and Hansen knocked off the top-seeded Manhattan team to reach the finals, and ALL six Rural players qualified for state.

This set the table for the 2003 state championship, only the second in school history. In order to win the state title, the Junior Blues got a sixth-place finish from Ben Wiechman and a seventh-place finish from Drew Hanson in singles. The doubles team of Sumeet Patel and Jeff Millberger finished second at state, and Trevor Hedberg and Matt Hansen finished ninth at state. The depth of the Junior Blues meant a lot of team points at state, and the championship trophy was captured.

2004—BACK TO BACK "SHIPS" FOR RURAL

With success usually comes inflated expectations—both from parents and fans. Some teams, some individuals handle it. Some embrace it. If anyone could keep a group grounded and focused, Kevin Hedberg is the coach who could do that.

The first hurdle was winning the thirteenth straight city tennis title. A good way to insure you have a shot to win that event is to make it to the finals in all four divisions. Rural got wins from Matt Hansen in number two singles, a victory in number one doubles from the team of Trevor Hedberg and Sumeet Patel, and a championship in number two doubles by Richard Lin and Ben Lepse. But even these victories didn't come easy. Two of the three events went three sets.

Hedberg spoke to the strength of the city saying, "The level (of play) is so good, there are so many good players right now in town. We didn't dominate, we just got by in some matches."

Even Rural's lone non-winner in number one singles, Drew Hanson, pushed the eventual champion, Joost from Shawnee Heights, hard. Hanson took the first set 6-4, but Joost bounced back with a 6-2 win and the match was called at 4-0 Joost due to Hanson's inability to continue and his withdrawal due to continual leg cramping.

It is worth noting that, after the city championship, the Junior Blues went to a fourteen-team invitational and finished second place behind Blue Valley Northwest by a slim two-point team difference.

Washburn Rural had to fight the other Centennial League teams and Emporia, Kansas's windy conditions that day, but Rural prevailed for their ninth straight league title, beating the other league schools AND the wind.

Rural got to the championship match in three of the four divisions and faced Hayden. The Junior Blues went 3-0 and Hayden 0-3, but they needed a little help from another school in the number one singles match which Hayden also reached. Shawnee Heights's Brandon Joost fended off Hayden's Sean McManus in a close 8-6 match which helped Rural win the team title over Hayden 25-19.

Drew Hansen captured the number two singles over his Hayden foe by a score of 8-2, and Washburn Rural continued their dominance in the doubles events. Patel and Hedberg beat the Hayden duo 6-2, 6-2 while the other Rural doubles team of Lin and Lepse defeated another pair from Hayden 8-6, capturing the number two doubles event.

Obviously both Hayden and Washburn Rural knew what was at stake as they faced off in three championships. "We maybe thought about them (the team standings) before the match, but once we got out and played, we were just trying to win," Ben Lepse told Brent Maycock. Capital-Journal sportswriter who covered the event for the local newspaper. Lepse also said, "I'm really enjoying this because we had to work really hard to make the top six." He was referring to the uphill battle to be in Rural's top six varsity spots.

There was one more step in the big three matches leading up to the state tournament. A tough regional field awaited Washburn Rural in Wichita, but the Junior Blues were experienced and up for the challenge. They swept three spots. In singles two teammates met for the championship, Drew Hansen and Matt Hanson. Drew won the match, so Rural finished number one and number two in singles. It was an exceptionally hot day, and Hedberg remembers his players suffering through a lot of cramping.

The doubles team of Patel and Hedberg had a tough challenge in the finals from a very good Manhattan tandem. They survived with a 6-3, 3-6, 6-1 victory to take first place. Capital-Journal sportswriter Brent Maycock's story lead about Patel and Hedberg was, "It took one smashed tennis racket, two very stern and heated talks from Washburn Rural coach Kevin Hedberg and three sets, but Sumeet Patel and Trevor Hedberg finally found their groove.

"We were frustrated," Patel told Maycock, "I don't think he's (Hedberg) ever been that mad (at me)."

The icing on the cake was a third-place finish by Lin and Lepse as they fought off a stiff test from a Wichita Southeast team 6-3, 3-6, 7-5. So, to defend their 2003 state title, the Junior Blues would take all six players to Emporia for the state tournament.

The Junior Blues rode the coattails of qualifying all six team members for the state event, and all of the players medaled. Matt Hansen and Drew Hanson finished fourth and sixth respectfully in singles. The doubles team of Patel and Hedberg finished third, and Lepse and Lin placed ninth. This gave Rural a narrow three-point cushion in team points as they captured back-to-back state championships—the third state title in boys tennis for the Junior Blues.

2005—DOES ONE DARE TO IMAGINE A THREEPEAT?

When your top four players return from back-to-back state championship runs, it's easy to get caught up in a flood of optimism. It's also easy to get complacent. Somewhere in between, Coach Hedberg probably wanted his players mindsets to fall. They needed the right amount of confidence, but an understanding that improving every day was crucial for them to stay ahead of the rest of the field.

The doubles team of Lin and Lepse had to be replaced, but the other pieces were there. Number one singles, Drew Hanson. Number two singles, Matt Hansen. And the strong doubles team of Sumeet Patel and Trevor Hedberg were back for one more run. The team looked very strong.

For the fourteenth straight year, the city teams met, and for the fourteenth straight year, the Junior Blues scored the most team points. In 2005, they swept all four divisions. A perfect score was more than Coach Hedberg could have hoped for, but left little doubt about the dominance of this program.

Ever gracious and humble, Hedberg told Capital-Journal sportswriter Rick Peterson, "There's so many good players in town that I'm surprised, but real pleased." Fourteen years of taking the city title can please anyone. "About five o'clock, I was just hoping for a win because it's a competitive thing and everybody comes ready."

Senior Drew Hanson came ready. In the last match of the day, he knocked off two-time state 5A champion Brandon Joost from Shawnee Heights by a score of 7-5, 7-5. Joost had previously won three straight city singles titles as well. This was Hanson's year however.

Hanson told sportswriter Peterson, "This gives me a lot of confidence going into the rest of the season. We still have a lot of hard meets left, so it's not over yet, but it's good to get that good win so you pick up some confidence." Ah, confidence. That tends to beat complacency.

Hanson also had a lot of previous success at the city meet with three city titles to his credit as well. He was part of the number one doubles championship duo his freshman year. His sophomore year, he claimed another title in number two singles, and the number one singles championship by unseating Joost this season.

The 2004 state championship doubles team of Patel and Hedberg won the number one doubles match over a Topeka West duo. The sophomore newcomer doubles team of Ben and Zach Newell earned first place in number two doubles with a 6-3, 6-1 win over a Hayden doubles team. Combine that with Matt Hansen's victory in number two singles as he defeated his Hayden foe 6-0, 6-0, and it was a clean city sweep for the Junior Blues who outdistanced second place Hayden by eleven team points, 32-21.

By the time the Centennial League event rolled around, the Junior Blues were without a key player from their top six. Matt Hansen opted to withdraw early from high school competition to pursue non-high school tennis competition in hopes to improve his chances for garnering a college scholarship. Ever the diplomat and advocate for his players, and one to support their decision if they think it's in their best interest, Hedberg gave him his blessing and moved on to replace him in the interest of team success—something the Junior Blues had had a lot of the previous two years. But losing a junior leader and a key contributor? Could Rural recover from that and have a chance to defend their previous two state titles?

Despite Height's Brandon Joost redeeming himself for dropping the city singles championship by winning the league singles championship over Drew Hanson, the Junior Blues still had enough fire power to win the league title over Hayden by a team score of 69-59.

The number one doubles team of Patel and Hedberg won their championship. It was the fourth league title for Sumeet Patel, and it was Trevor Hedberg's third. The Newell brothers, Zach and Ben, took third in doubles, and another Centennial League banner could hang from the rafters of the school's gym. In a 25-year span dating back to 1981, Rural's boys' tennis had captured twenty-three league championships. A quarter of a century, and only two years Rural failed to win their league. Again, confidence booster. Traditions.

One more step to state. Regionals would be in Topeka at Kossover Courts. Washburn Rural managed to win their seventh straight regional title taking fifteen team points to the closest contender, Manhattan's five points.

Drew Hanson captured the regional singles title and then told Capital-Journal's Rick Peterson, "I've always said, 'Let's go out on a high note.'" He defeated his Wichita Southeast opponent 6-3, 6-2 for his high note. In an all-Washburn Rural doubles final, teammates Patel and Hedberg defeated the Newell brothers, Zach and Ben. The first and second-place finish in doubles combined with Hanson's first-place singles finish was enough to propel the Junior Blues to their seventh straight regional title.

Hanson—who would take a 22-2 record to state singles—talked about what had occurred the past two seasons for Rural, saying, "We've won it the last two years as a team, and this year we are trying to focus more on the individual stuff and let the team thing happen. It's our senior year for me, Sumeet and Trevor, and we want this pretty bad." Hanson clarified the *individual stuff*, saying, "They want the doubles, and I want the singles, and we just figure if we focus on our own games, then the team's going to come together."

Patel said that he and Hedberg, now 25-1, also saw good things ahead of them at the state championship the following weekend. "I think we're playing really well right now," Patel said, "We're both hitting our shots where we want to. We're feeling our groove with our shots. We're really confident with our strokes right now. I think we have a pretty good shot at competing for a state title."

So how was Coach Hedberg feeling after three years of major wins and successes? Ever the one to keep perspective, he reflected, "I felt good about how the boys played." He added, "I think we struggled down the stretch a little, just in terms of being tired. All my kids are good students, and it's important to them that they do well in school, and it's hard when you're gone from class to play tennis." How about a nice dose of perspective as your sports team pursues something really special. School still and always is the priority.

That pursuit had some odd twists and turns, but consistency won out. Drew Hanson held up his end of the team scoring by winning the state singles championship. Patel and Hedberg ran their record to 29-1 and also captured the state doubles championship. Washburn Rural, quietly and methodically, won their third straight state championship. They overcame losing one of their top six players midway into the season, while a pair of sophomore brothers grabbed valuable points along the way and became a force to be reckoned with themselves.

Historically, somewhere in the state of Kansas, there may be another three-peats in tennis but maybe not in a program that also owned the length of tennis dominance in their city and in their league. Coach Kevin Hedberg had to be proud. How much better to have your son on the championship teams? Confidence vs. Complacency. Yep, confidence won. And hard work along the way kept the tennis players fit and skilled. Junior Blue tennis has a special quality attached to it, and the only thing that changes year-to year are the players and the lineups. Because Hedberg never ages.

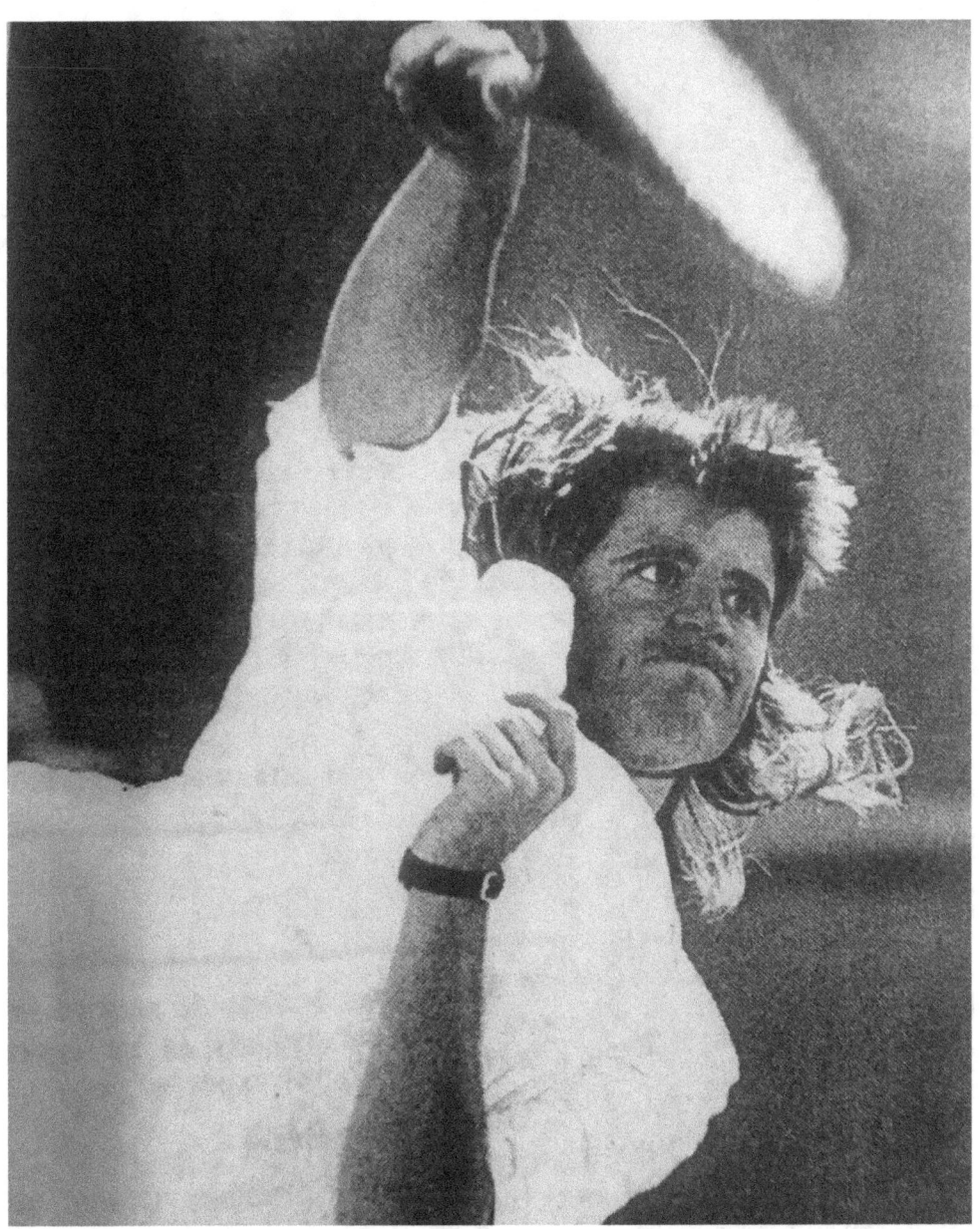

Ryan Kuhn, returning senior in 1994, placed 3rd in doubles at 1993 state tournament.

(Top) Brian Hejtmanek was a sophomore in 1994 when he captured the Topeka city championship's number one singles. That year won their 14th Centennial League title in 15 years.

(Bottom) Wes Geier returns a volley at the '97 Centennial League tournament. He and Mike Alva captured the #2 doubles championship.

1994 Kirk Stewart serves against St. Thomas Aquinas at the Washburn Rural Invitational, one of seven events the Junior Blues won that season.

Key contributors in 1996 Danny Williams and Todd Thelen
(Photo credit: *Topeka Capital-Journal*)

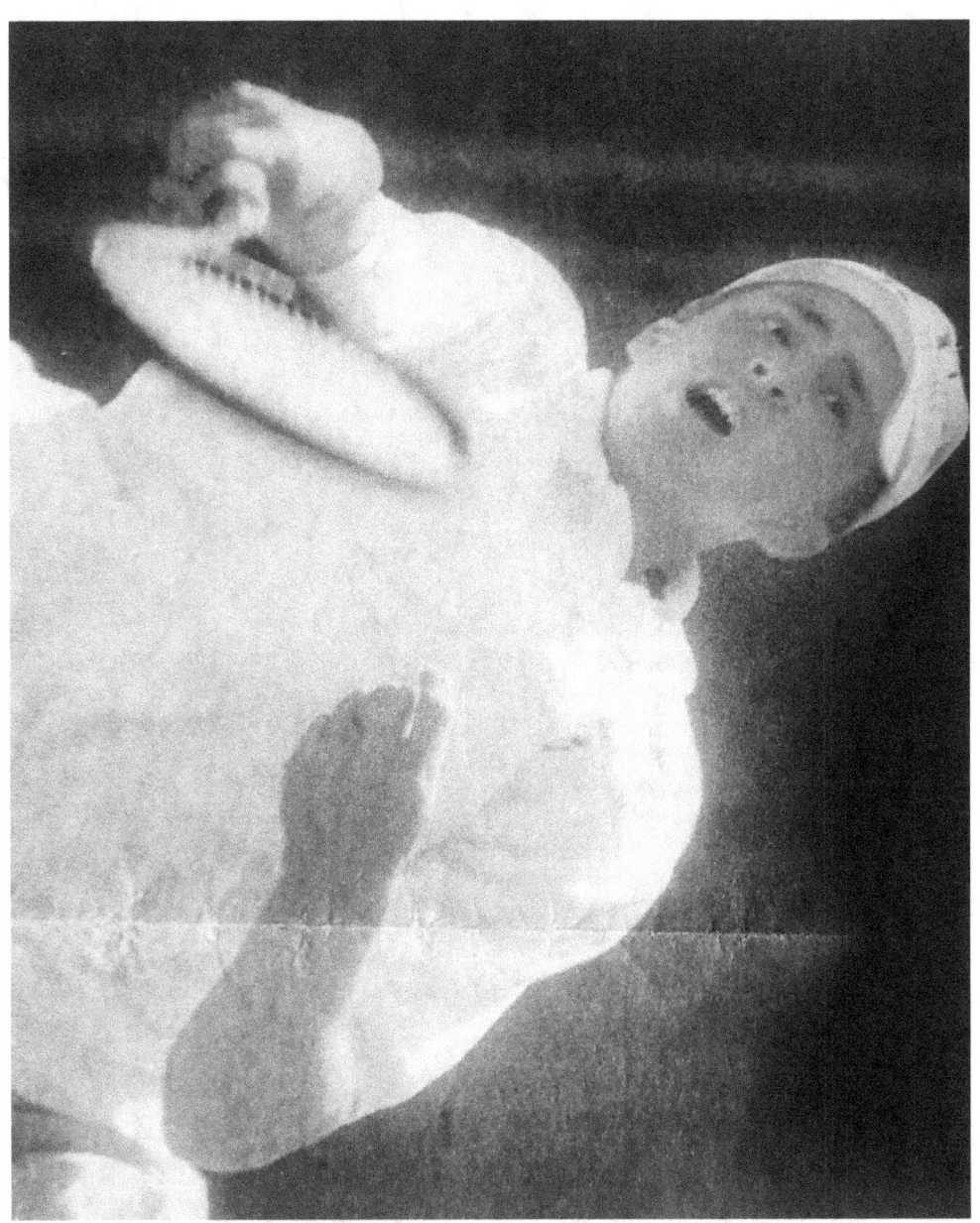

Justin Keller helped Rural to their sixth straight city championship in 1997 capturing the number one singles event in an 8-3 victory over Hayden's Suddarth

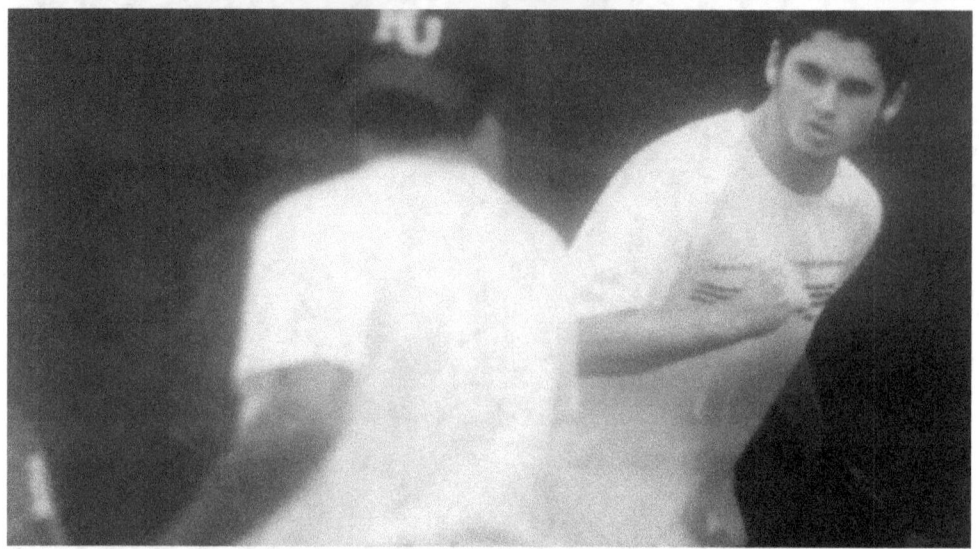

(Top) Senior David Stauffer in the 2000 state tournament. Stauffer finished with a 23-4 record leading Rural to a 3rd place team finish. Stauffer went on to play tennis at Kansas University.
(Photo credit: *Topeka Capital-Journal*)

(Bottom) During 2003 Topeka city championship the doubles team Sumeet Patel and Trevor Hedberg celebrate their event win as well as the 13th consecutive city title for Rural.

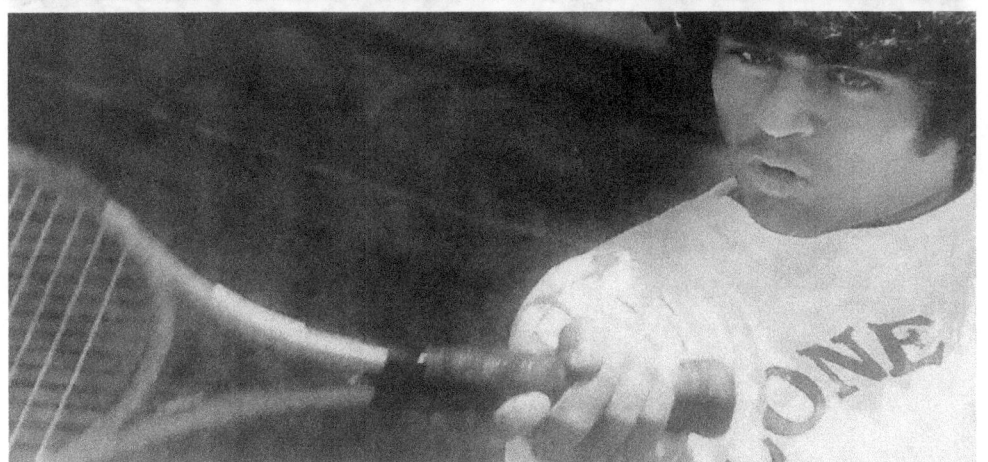

(Top) Senior Drew Hanson knocked off three time city champion Brandon Joost of Shawnee Heights at the 2005 city meet.

(Bottom) Sumeet Patel helping the Junior Blues to their 7th straight regional title in 2005. Patel and Hedberg's were doubles champions beating their 2nd place teammates Ben and Zach Newell.

(Photo credit: *Topeka Capital-Journal*)

In 2006 Hedberg juggled the lineup to help WR win their 15th straight city title. Jason Lepse unselfishly played doubles instead of singles. WR beat Topeka High 30-21.

(Photo credit: *Topeka Capital-Journal*)

Zach Newell makes a return against the other WR doubles team at the 2006 league tournament. The Newell brothers captured the number one doubles.

(Photo credit: *Topeka Capital-Journal*)

(Top) Ben Newell returning a volley during the 2007 Centennial League tournament. Newell and Zach Newell defeated their teammates and runners up teammates Jason Lepse and Bronson Brassel giving WR their 12th straight league team championship.

(Bottom) Twins Zach and Ben Newell as seniors winning their city event in 2007 helping Rural to their 16th straight city title

In 2012 Scott Ziegler and Griffin Koupal won the number one doubles at city meet, Rural's 21st city championship in a row.

(Photo credit: *Topeka Capital-Journal*)

Bobby Florence (left) makes a return as his partner Max Cooper looks on. Florence and Cooper won the league doubles championship helping Rural win their 15th straight Centennial League team title in 2010.

(Photo credit: *Topeka Capital-Journal*)

2011 Centennial League singles champion Daniel de Zamacona drives a backhand to his opponent. He ended up beating his teammate, Connor Edwards 6-4,7-5 for a one, two finish.

(Photo credit: *Topeka Capital-Journal*)

(Top) Kyle Beard on his way to a city doubles championship in 2015 which was Rural's 23rd title in the previous 24 years. The team title was a 30-19 win over Seaman.

(Bottom) At 2018 city championship Max Cassidy won his second consecutive single title helping Rural to another city team title. Cassidy was coming off a winter ankle injury.

2019 freshman Mason Thieu makes a return in the city number one singles match. Thieu took second and helped Rural win their 27th city championship in the last 28 years.

2006—WHAT DO YOU DO TO FOLLOW-UP THREE CONSECUTIVE STATE CHAMPIONSHIPS

The nucleus of the success for the previous three seasons graduated in the spring, but Rural was still able to be a very dominant team the year after in 2006.

The 2006 version of the Junior Blues was able to juggle its lineup and find ways to win the city, league, and regional titles in 2006. They were strong enough to come away with third place at state after winning three straight tournaments. Rural had been dominant at the state level dating back to 1999 when it finished second. In 2000, the team was third place, and in 2001 captured second place. They then placed third place in 2002 before finishing first in 2003, 2004 and 2005, and again third place in 2006. Try and wrap your head around that.

In Rick Peterson's Capital-Journal article about the city tennis event, the focus was on the Washburn Rural dominance in this annual event. Peterson's lead paragraph spoke to the fact that Kevin Hedberg knew that the incredible winning streak would end one day. "Thursday wasn't that day," Peterson reported.

On that Thursday, Rural won three of four events, outdistancing second place Topeka High by a score of 30-21 for the boys' fifteenth straight city championship.

"The streak has kind of taken on a life of its own, and each team doesn't want to give it up," Hedberg said. "Somebody will—we're going to lose at some point, and it could be next year—but each team kind of takes it on."

After graduating three state champions, this looked like it could have been the year, but some juggling of who competed for the Junior Blue in each of the four events made a difference. Junior Ben Newell, who usually played doubles, won the city singles championship beating a Topeka West player 6-4, 7-5.

Sophomore Jason Lepse, who usually plays singles, joined Ben Newell's doubles partner, brother Zach Newell to win the number one doubles title. Andy Brownback and Bronson Brassel won the number two doubles crown, and Senior Blake Baraban finished second in the number two singles event.

"I don't think they would have let me play less than what I thought our best chance (to win) was," Hedberg commented on the lineup changes. "When I mentioned it to them in practice, no one questioned it. They all endorsed it and then went out and made it work. We looked at our lineup looking at the strength of the field. Topeka High is a very good team and a deep team, and they really worried us. Today we just felt like, point-wise, this was the way to go." That's that team-side of Kansas high school tennis, and nobody understands it and plays better to their strengths than Kevin Hedberg.

Ben Newell would be back in doubles for Rural's next meet but was glad to take advantage of a rare chance to play singles at the city meet. Newell said, "Actually, I like singles. It's just that the competition there is a lot harder. I play doubles with my brother, and we just beat the team that was third at state last year, so we're doing pretty well there. We'll definitely stay with doubles. We just picked a lineup that would work for us here. All of us were talking about how this one might be the only one we lose, but we ended up almost sweeping it."

In 2006, the Centennial League changed the format of scoring for the event. Even then, the Junior Blues captured their eleventh straight title. The new format was to accommodate the addition of four more teams to the league which made the total number of teams ten. Added to the league field were Junction City, Manhattan, Topeka High and Topeka West. It became the league with all the city teams plus Emporia, Junction City and Manhattan. All singles and doubles teams played six matches, so the tournament was about eight hours long. That lengthy play didn't bother Washburn Rural.

Zach Newell, who captured the number one doubles event with his brother Ben, said, "This is the first time I've experienced something like this. I've never actually played this much before, but this was a fun day for all of us."

"It was very demanding," Rural coach Kevin Hedberg said. "It was very much a regional type of thing where you're grinding for a long time."

The Junior Blues also got fourth and fifth-place finishes from their singles players, Jason Lepse and Blake Barabon. They used a fourth-place finish from Andy Brownback and Bronson Brassel to take the team title by an 85-73 margin over Topeka High.

"I'm thrilled," Hedberg said. "I've kind of downplayed (this team) and underplayed them all year and said we're not as good and all this other stuff. Actually, they've become a very good team and real solid. I couldn't be more proud of them."

Solid enough that they captured their eighth straight regional championship and took a good contingency to the state tournament.

The Capital-Journal downplayed their chances of winning a fourth straight, but Hedberg was okay with that based on the results of the season thus far. "They've exceeded my expectations already. I'm tickled with them," Hedberg said. Pointing toward a bright future and a continuation of good tennis at Washburn Rural, Hedberg added, "We're a young team. Other than senior Andy Brownback, everybody comes back next year, and we've got a good freshmen class and good underclassmen already here, so this is a good building year for us."

Hedberg went on to comment about their chances at state this way, "There's five schools with the same amount of entries and, as far as entry position (based on regional results), our position is probably weakest among the five."

Ever the prognosticator, Hedberg said it was realistic for the Junior Blues to shoot for a top three finish. And that's just what they got based on the doubles championship by the undefeated Newell brothers, Zach and Ben. Rural did capture third place as a team which was a pretty good achievement to follow up the three straight state championships. The Newell brothers remained undefeated for the season.

2007—HOW DO YOU FOLLOW THREE STATE CHAMPIONSHIPS AND A THIRD PLACE AT STATE

How about a trifecta of city, league and regional champions? That seemed like a pretty solid plan or goal for the season to follow up such an unprecedented four-year run of success.

The trick was to keep a roster of forty-three tennis players happy. That's a lot of tennis courts, and that was the number Coach Hedberg was faced with at the start of the 2007 season. Hedberg started with his predetermined "rank order" of all players, and he passed out the players' rank and order with this caveat at the top of the page:

"This is our starting ladder. The rotation works like this: We start from the bottom with even numbers. They can challenge up 1 or 3 slots. If they win, players switch places. The next challenge begins with the lowest odd number with players able to challenge up 1 or 3 slots. The next challenge begins with #3 position and works downward with odd numbered players getting to challenge 1 to 3 slots. The last challenge cycle begins with position #2 and works downward with even number players getting to challenge up 1 to 3 slots." That's how you give all forty-plus their chance(s). It ends up being a "who beats who" venture. Pretty hard to argue with that. It may be the most ingenious way for sorting out your top players when there was an abundance of players vying for spots on the team. Fortunately, Hedberg said, they did not have to use it often.

The city championship streak extended to sixteen years in a row. The boys realized the importance of the streak to their coach, and they took pride in that annual challenge.

"We're aware of it and we're not going to let it end, not this year anyway," senior Zach Newell told Capital-Journal sports reporter Rick Peterson after the Junior Blues beat the second-place finishers Shawnee Heights and Topeka High by a team score of 28 to 20. Newell added, "Coach Hedberg is always real modest and acts like he doesn't care about the streak, but we all think he does. He gets real nervous for it."

The nervousness subsided when Rural placed finalists in three of the four events and then went on to win those three divisions. The twins, Zach and Ben Newell, won the number-one doubles crown. Bronson Brassel and Jason Lepse won the number-two doubles event. Freshman Johnny Stueve won the number two singles title in his first attempt. Sebastien Reiter took a fourth place finish in number-one singles.

Hedberg said, "I always worry a lot. We've got so many good young players coming in (at city high schools) now, and I never take any of those guys for granted. There's so many good players now that don't care if you won last year or ever." Tennis is about the current players, the current season.

By the end of the event, Hedberg was able to breathe a little easier. He told the Capital-Journal's Peterson, "We played real well. This has been a screwy season, I think for all of us with the rainouts and the shorter season, so I think we're all trying to get enough playing time." A particularly major concern when your squad numbers forty-plus players.

In the Centennial League event, the Junior Blues captured first and second-place in doubles, and in singles, finished third and fourth as the team defeated rival Hayden by the team score of 91-72.

"Our singles players showed up and played well and have done nothing but help themselves today for the regional, and our doubles teams played real well, so it's been a good day," Hedberg reflected in the Capital-Journal. He told reporter Rick Peterson, "We wanted to send everybody home tired, but happy. I don't know if we can do it any different because I think the format is really good, but you worry on a day when it's 88 degrees—and they're not used to it—that they're going to hit the wall at some point."

The Junior Blues capped their season with another regional win—their ninth in a row dating back to 1999. And then they won the 6A state championship for the fourth time in five years, riding the coat tails of the Newell brothers finishing third place at state in doubles and their teammates Brandon Brassel and Jason Lepse finishing in fourth place. Johnny Stueve placing at state as a freshman provided a much-needed boost in points to accomplish this. Four state championships in the last five years. Can everyone say dominance?

2008—DO THEY FEEL THE PRESSURE TO DO WELL?

Old habits are hard to break. Washburn Rural marched to their seventeenth straight city championship. They had to rely on the boys capturing first place in three of the four events. They outdistanced second-place Shawnee Heights 29 to 19.

The one event they won went, once again, to Seaman's Steven Fletcher as he defended his singles crown from the previous year.

Hedberg told Capital-Journal sportswriter Rick Peterson that, "They were all asking me about the number (of consecutive city titles), but we didn't talk about it—we never talk about it."

Regardless, Hedberg's efforts to ignore or downplay the streak didn't mean that he or his team didn't shoot to win this event. They aimed for this every year as one of the three or four most important matches. Bragging rights in your city mean something.

Jason Lepse and Bronson Brassel captured the number one doubles championship. The other doubles team of Conner Edwards and Daniel de Zamacona won the number two doubles event. Bobby Florence won the number two singles event, and Johnny Stueve placed fourth in number one singles. Those placings carried them to the team title.

The Centennial League title was almost a repeat of the city. Rural rolled right into the regionals on a high note.

At the regional event, it was business as usual, and Rural won its tenth straight regional title. The doubles teams led the way. Brassel and Lepse took first place 6-4, 6-4 in defeating their teammates Edwards and de Zamacona who took second place. In the singles event, Johnny Stueve took second place, and Florence finished third.

"It was a good day," Hedberg told Capital-Journal reporter Austin Meek. "It's always nice to get everybody in (to state) because it's fun to make the trip, and it increases your chances of being able to score some points in the state tournament."

Brassel commented on his doubles partner, Jason Lepse, "I thought Jason played really well. It was nice to play our own team in the finals." Both of Edwards and de Zamacona's only losses that year came at the hands of their teammates. Sickness and injury may have slowed down the progress of Edwards and de Zamacona or they would have been playing at an even higher level. If that's possible. "They haven't gotten to play that much together. They can get better (as a doubles team) before the state tournament."

At the state tournament, the doubles teams fared well. Edwards and de Zamacona finished sixth at state and completed a 22-4 overall seasonal record. Lepse and Brassel placed seventh at state and sported a 28-5 record. Bobby Florence gained valuable experience winning a match at state and finished a good singles season at 21-5. Johnny Stueve finished the season 23-11 and earned a tenth-place medal at state. The team finished third for another piece of hardware for their trophy case. Four championships and two *thirds* in the last six years.

2009—A SEASON THAT HAD A LOT TO LIVE UP TO

When you look back at the previous ten seasons, you see four state championships, nine regional championships, and ten city and league titles. That tells you the kind of expectations you put on yourself as a member of the Washburn Rural varsity tennis team. One of Coach Hedberg's challenges was to motivate continued success without making it overwhelming for the tennis players.

The 2009 tennis team met the challenge of the city streak head on. They took three of the four events. This propelled Rural to the eighteenth consecutive city team victory. Most of the players who competed this season weren't even born yet when the streak started. The Junior Blues outscored second-place Hayden 29-19. Shawnee Heights and Topeka West were tied for third with 18 apiece.

Not even a rainstorm, that pushed the meet indoors, could slow down Rural. Senior Branson Brassel and sophomore Conner Edwards captured first place in number one doubles competition. Sophomore Daniel De Zamacona won the number two singles event. Juniors Bobby Florence and Max Cooper took the crown in number two doubles. Junior Johnny Stueve took third place in a tough number one singles field.

Hedberg said after the meet, "We had a good week. We played really well at Emporia Tuesday night, and I think we kind of kept it going today. Those guys playing number one singles are tough, and any time you play them it's going to be rough. Johnny played better against them today—didn't' win, but played a lot better. And the other guys are just getting better and better all the time. I'm real pleased with how we are playing."

A Capital-Journal sports reporter covering the Centennial League meet, pointed out that senior Branson Brassel has never been on a Rural team that has lost a city championship, nor a league championship or even dropped a regional championship. In fact, his past three years the Junior Blues finished in the top three at state. After Washburn Rural won the Centennial League meet, Brassel started to realize how special all that experience had been for him.

After the Junior Blues won the league title—winning 90-66 over Shawnee Heights—Brassel reflected, "My first three years, freshman through junior year, I definitely took it for granted. But now I'm a senior, I'm kind of realizing all of our accomplishments, and you don't want to be the senior that all the streaks end on."

Tuning up for a run at the eleventh regional championship, Brassel and doubles teammate Edwards set the table for winning the league title by winning the doubles event. Florence and Cooper finished third in doubles competition. Stueve and De Zamacona took third and fourth respectively in the singles competition.

Rural marched to another regional title—its eleventh straight. Brassel and Edwards won the doubles event. Cooper and Florence finished second to their teammates. Daniel de Zamacoma won the singles event, beating his teammate Stueve in the finals. Stueve finished second.

There would not be a top three team finish at 6A state however, but Brassel and Edwards finished fifth in doubles. Cooper and Florence finished sixth at state in doubles. Daniel de Zamacona finished in a tie for ninth place in singles along with his teammate Stueve. Their team total had them finishing fourth in 6A. Close, and a very respectable season indeed.

The 2009 edition of the Junior Blue boys' tennis program captured the seventeenth consecutive city championship and thirteenth consecutive league team title. Additionally, they won their tenth straight regional championship and placed fourth as a team at the state tournament. I'd say they measured up quite well.

By 2009, the boys tennis team had more team state championships than any other sport at Washburn Rural (5). As far as individual champions at state, they boasted three singles championships and four doubles state championships.

HEDBERG REFLECTS ON HIS SECOND DECADE OF TENNIS AT RURAL 2000-09

Hedberg says that while the 90's established some norms, in the 2000's there was a precedence about playing high school and then college. In fact, the trend carried into the 2015 teams when nearly all six of the top players went on to attend college and play college tennis. Many of them had great careers.

It was also these years that would see the most consistent success at the state level. One never knows for certain, but with just a bit of better fortune, the boys might have captured five out of ten state championships between 2000-2010. A very likely scenario with just a bit of different circumstances involving injuries and who participated in post-season each year.

But all that would have changed was history. Playing tennis at Washburn Rural was always rewarding in its own right.

Hedberg also mentioned the dominance witnessed from Johnson County tennis. He stated that, between 2003 and 2014, the 6A state champion came from a Johnson County school ten of those seasons.

2010—NINETEEN CONSECUTIVE CITY TITLES: FIFTEEN STRAIGHT CENTENNIAL LEAGUE TITLES

As a team, the boys won their nineteenth consecutive city championship. They also ran their streak of Centennial League championships to fifteen consecutive years. Impressive as those local accomplishments are, they also won their twelfth straight regional title. The season culminated with a 6A state tournament third place finish. This was becoming habitual.

At the city event, Rural took three first places out of four events. They outscored second place Shawnee Heights, who undoubtedly had the best singles player that year in Chance Joost. Max Cooper and Bobby Florence won the number one doubles event. The other doubles team of Jake Long and Simon Beatty took home the first place in number two doubles. Daniel de Zamacona won the number two singles division. Connor Edwards placed third in number one singles in a very good field of singles players.

When asked about the string of nineteen straight by Capital-Journal sportswriter Rick Peterson, Hedberg said, "You feel fortunate. My team this year is a bunch of hard-working guys that put in a lot of time so, it's a nice reward for them. Every year is a different year, and it's going to end at some point. You just do the best you can each year and play."

The Centennial League event had all components of Good, Bad and the Ugly. The Junior Blues took their fifteenth straight league title. That was good. The bad was that one of the best freshmen in the state and his doubles partner had to default in the semifinals. The ugly was the freshman Beatty, who unfortunately broke his leg.

Max Cooper told Capital-Journal sportswriter Rick Peterson that, "It (the injury) shakes you up a little bit but you've just got to play through it. You can't worry about it, you've got to worry about what you're doing. Once you're off the court, then you can start to worry about it."

Coach Hedberg looked at it matter-of-fact. "You don't replace arguably the best freshman in Kansas. You don't replace him, but we'll do our best."

The doubles team of Florence and Cooper took first place in doubles. With the default, Beatty and Long took fourth. Edwards worked his way to the singles finals only to face one of the best, Shawnee Heights Chance Joost. And de Zamacona placed third in singles. Rural took the bittersweet league championship, outdistancing Topeka West 90-68.

Without missing a beat—but definitely missing Beatty—Washburn Rural brought their 'A' game to regionals and won their twelfth straight regional. Rural junior Edwards picked a good time to win his first singles event that season, and he met teammate de Zaracona in the finals. Additionally, Cooper and Florence won the doubles championship. Long and Ziegler, pairing up for the doubles due to Beatty's injury, finished fourth. Rural once again was taking their whole team to state, and during a year that their best player was sidelined.

The Junior Blue boys were very confident that they could make a good showing at state. Hedberg, who didn't want to add any lofty expectations, said, "We're playing well and we've got a good team. We know exactly what we're looking at when we go to Kansas City (location of the 6A state tournament). We know how hard that is and how tough it is. Hopefully, we'll bring back a trophy, but if we don't and play well, that's life." He meant every word of that statement. When you focus on playing well vs. winning, winning kind of takes care of itself.

At the 6A state tournament, Rural ended up with two entries in the semifinals. But, due to rain, Saturday's final day was pushed to Monday. Edwards made it to the semifinals, as did the doubles duo of Cooper and Florence. Singles player de Zamacona was still alive in the consolation bracket.

After the delay, Edwards ended up with a fourth-place finish. Cooper and Florence placed third, and de Zamacona came back to finish fifth at state. As a team, Rural finished third place and brought home a trophy. Good sometimes comes to those who work diligently. Consistency does get rewarded quite often.

Conner Edwards posted a 29-6 singles record. Edwards was third at city in number one singles, second at league and first at regionals. He finished fourth at state in singles.

Daniel De Zamacona finished first in number two singles at city, third in singles at league and second in singles at regionals. He went to state and finished fifth-place.

The 2010 season saw the doubles team of Bobby Florence and Max Cooper finish with a 33-2 record. Their career record was 59-11. They won the number one doubles event at city, league, regionals and placed third at the 6A state tournament.

Jake Long and Simon Beatty held a 25-0 record, capturing first place in city number two doubles and were fourth at the Centennial League tournament.

Long paired with Scott Ziegler as they captured fourth in the regional tournament, and the doubles team scored a point at the state tournament, which helped Rural earn third place as a team.

One can't help but wonder, if Beatty hadn't have suffered a season ending injury combined with his dual success against Blue Valley North, could Washburn Rural have claimed yet another state title? There would be a good case made that they could have.

2011—THE GRADUATION OF THE MOST SUCCESSFUL DOUBLES DUO

Conner Edwards and Daniel de Zamacona really distinguished themselves. Impressively, both Connor and Daniel were all-city and all-league selections all four years. The two posted the highest state finishes combined in the history of Washburn Rural tennis. The record they broke was theirs from the previous year when they were juniors. As juniors, they finished fourth and second, combining for twenty-five team points. They surpassed David Stauffer and Justin Keller, who combined for eighteen team points in 1999. The other tandem of note was the 1996 pair of Brian Hejtmanek and Danny Williams, who finished fifth and sixth at their state competitions respectively.

Conner finished with a final record of 114-23 and Daniel was 108-26.

Additionally, as a team, the boys ran their string of city championships to twenty in a row. Their league dominance saw them winning their sixteenth consecutive league championship and their thirteenth straight regional title and once again finished third at the 6A state event. In a fifteen-year stretch from 1999-2011, Washburn Rural took six third-place team finishes at state, two second-place finishes and won four state titles. Consistency.

The doubles team of Zach Aldrich and Scott Ziegler placed eighth at the state tournament and finished with an overall 23-9 record. They took second place at city in number one doubles, first place in league doubles and second place in doubles at regionals. Both were named to the all-city and all-league team.

The doubles team of Zach Madel and Griff Koupal finished first in city number two doubles. They placed fourth in doubles at the league event and third in regionals, and finished with a 20-10 record.

2012—ABLE TO KEEP THE CITY AND LEAGUE STREAK LED BY ZIEGLER AND KOUPAL

Rural once again captured the city and the league team titles by slim margins. So going into regionals, they looked to be contenders, but Hedberg was cautious because of the close calls at city and league.

At the city championship, the doubles first-place sweep by Griff Koupal and Scott Ziegler and the team of Reid Osborn and Matt Murray combined with a third-place finish by Connor Farron in number two singles to set up a 24-20 team victory over Topeka West. Topeka High and Seaman scored nineteen points. It was a close call for Rural.

Hedberg was asked about the string of twenty-one straight city championships and what it would be like if they didn't finish first. Hedberg said, "Losing it is going to happen. It's gonna happen and, when it does happen, I don't want them to feel like they have failed because every year's new. I just want them to compete hard and enjoy the sport. It was by no means easy, and our league meet on Monday will be absolutely insane and everything could roll over and be completely different." A level-headed coach, like Hedberg, can put it all in perspective.

But Rural won Monday's league event for their seventeenth straight championship. Koupal and Ziegler took care of business and won the doubles event. The sophomore doubles team of Osborn and Murray finished third in doubles. Farron finished seventh in singles, and Eric Seals finished eighth to establish an 80-68 margin over second-place Seaman and Topeka West.

Hedberg told Capital-Journal sportswriter Rick Peterson, "Nothing's different (about regionals) than it was last Thursday or Monday (city and league events). I've got to tell you, it's been fun because those kids have done everything I've asked them to, and I think they are finally getting it and they want to be good and they're going to work at it. That parts been very enjoyable." Not only did Hedberg enjoy the successes, he enjoyed the experiences, enjoyed his team.

Ziegler and Koupal continued their hot play by completing the trifecta of city, league and regional champions in doubles. They ran their season record to 28-2 while beating their teammates Osborn and Murray who placed second. Farron finished fifth in singles as Washburn Rural took the team title by a 17-13 margin over Manhattan. Griff Koupal had this to say about his and Ziegler's success this season, "Scotty and I have played well for the last couple of weeks so we really just wanted to keep that momentum continuing. Our goal is to keep it going and planning on improving for state next week."

At state, Koupal and Ziegler were knocked into the consolation round, but made the best of it by taking three 9-3 consolation matches and finishing fifth place at state. They finished the season with a 32-3 record. As a team, Rural finished ninth place. Hedberg told Capital-Journal sportswriter Scott Paske, "We've been kind of a young team in terms of experience, and Scott Ziegler has been a good leader for us. He's so relaxed and just has fun playing. He enjoys what he does and that makes Griff play better. I'm pleased with how they came around."

2013—END OF AN IMPRESSIVE STREAK, BUT THE SUN DOES CAME UP AGAIN

The coach in Kevin Hedberg knew that all good streaks must eventually come to an end, but none of the teams wanted it to be their year. Hayden beat Washburn Rural by a mere point to end the city championship streak at twenty-one. That is *twenty-one* straight years—over two decades of dominance in a city that has seven high schools.

Hayden's winning coach had this nice tribute to pay respects to Washburn Rural's boys tennis program. "They're the best," Hayden's coach James Sandstrom told Capital-Journal sportswriter Rick Peterson. He went on to say, "They're the model, they're the program that everybody wants to be like and that's what we push for, try to be like Rural."

Even though Washburn Rural won both doubles events, they fell a point short in their bid for twenty-two straight years. The Hunter brothers captured the two singles events for Hayden, but it was the fourth place finish by Hayden's doubles team of Beck and Federico that ensured the city team title for Hayden.

Rural captured the number one doubles event with senior Griff Koupal and junior Matt Murrray. Their teammates, junior Reid Osborn and freshman Nathan Osborn, took the number two doubles event.

Coach Hedberg was not surprised that the team title was won by a mere point. "It was a bit of a perfect storm, and we knew coming in that we didn't have much margin for error." Hedberg graciously conceded, "Hayden deserves it, and they won it and we'll come back Monday at the league meet and see if we can't do just a little bit better. I told my wife last night, it's win by one, tie or lose by one, and we lost by one (point)."

On the following Monday, the seven city schools were joined by out-of-town league schools Emporia, Junction City and Manhattan. Once again, the strength of the doubles teams helped Rural win its eighteenth straight league title, taking a bit of the sting out of losing the city crown.

Rural added two top-ten finishes in singles at league, with freshman Tanner Driggers posting a fifth-place finish and senior Eric Seals finishing ninth in singles. This gave Rural the team title beating Hayden 81-67. It took a solid team effort with everybody contributing to keep the league title and trophy in Rural's trophy case.

"I thought this was our best team effort," Hedberg told Capital-Journal sportswriter Rick Peterson. "I'm really happy for my singles players—fifth out of Tanner and ninth for Eric. An 8-4 record by our singles players is awfully good."

Koupal and Murray defeated their teammates, the Osborns, for a first and second-place finish in doubles. Koupal said, "We were optimistic. After the city meet Thursday (the goal) was just to come back and play as well or better as we did before, and we knew if we played hard enough we could get this." Koupal went on to give credit to his teammates who played singles. "Seals and Driggers played incredibly well today," Koupal said. "They did more than we could have asked for. They had the toughest draw, and they're out here playing some of the toughest guys in the state."

The Washburn Rural Junior Blues went on to capture their fifteenth straight regional championship.

At the 6A state meet, the undefeated doubles team of Koupal and Murray lost their first match of the season, dropping them into the consolation side of the bracket. The Blue Valley doubles team won over Koupal and Murray, 6-4, 4-6 and 10-8 in a super tie-breaker.

The doubles team of the Osborns, who were 24-2 entering the tournament, lost their first match, won the second, but with a loss in the third were out of the tournament on Friday.

"I'd be a liar to say I wasn't disappointed, but I wasn't disappointed in the effort," Hedberg said of the Junior Blues overall showing. "I live in the real world, and I know just how good those Kansas City schools are. I've been watching them all season, and I knew what we were in for. I'm glad Koupal and Murray are playing in the morning (Saturday)."

On Saturday, Koupal and Murray placed ninth in the state doubles event. Murray said, "We tried to forget about our (first-round losses) and do our best in our next matches. It feels great to end the season with a win." As a team, Rural finished in a ninth place tie with Hutchinson.

At the end-of-the-year banquet, Coach Hedberg recognized the individuals but then knew how to take a little bit of the sting out of the city streak ending. Hedberg talked about the rich tradition of tennis at Rural. He mentioned that the boys tennis program has thirty-one Centennial League titles out of thirty-four years. He pointed out that it was the most of any other boys sport at Washburn Rural, and also mentioned the girls tennis team had twenty-six league titles. He pointed out that the five state championships the boys tennis teams had earned put them on the top of all other Rural sports for state championships.

He spelled out what it takes to reach and sustain this level of excellence. He told those at the banquet, parents and participants, "It is not complicated really, but it is not easy." He mentioned that, as a goal, they may want to be on the courts playing tennis three hundred times a year. But if three hundred is not possible, shoot for two hundred and fifty. He emphasized the importance of playing in addition to impressing upon his players and their parents, the importance of drills and private lessons. "You can not buy excellence, but you can earn it."

2014—GOING TO START A NEW CITY STREAK: LEAGUE STREAK ENDS

There are two things to know about winning streaks. The longer they go the more impressive they are. However, they ultimately will end at some point, and 2013 was the year for Rural's city championship streak to end—at the hand of Hayden High School.

In 2014, their consecutive win streak at the Centennial League meet would also end.

Early in the season, Washburn Rural had a quad with three other league schools, Manhattan, Topeka High and Topeka West, and Rural dominated that meet. The Junior Blues won eleven of twelve matches on the day and went 3-0. The doubles teams won all their matches. In number one doubles, Reid Osborn and Nathan Osborn won all three matches, as did the number two doubles team of Brenden Garland and Kyle Beard. Their number two singles player, Jordan Lind, also went 3-0. Number one singles player, Matt Murray, went 2-1, dropping a match 8-1 to a very good Manhattan player.

Hedberg told Capital-Journal sportswriter Rick Peterson, "The kids are playing well, they're working hard and they like each other. It's been good, and going from here, we'll see where it takes us." In coach speak that might be interpreted as a coach citing the positives to a season that they aren't totally certain what can be achieved.

Hedberg had depth this year with about nine players capable and ready to see varsity time. "I'd say we could go nine (at the varsity level) right now, and I'm probably not giving my younger ones the benefit of the doubt," he commented. "We've got another two weeks before I have to make real difficult decisions (about who plays varsity)," Hedberg acknowledged.

Washburn Rural returned to business as usual, winning the city event and starting a new streak after Hayden beat them in 2013. However, it was Hayden again this year who were streak-breakers, halting Rural's Centennial League dominance at eighteen straight team titles.

With the two Hunters from Hayden finishing first and second place in singles, it placed a lot of Rural's emphasis on the doubles event. Washburn Rural's duo of Murray and Nathan Osborn came through with a doubles championship, so it came down to the other doubles team. Because of an academic conflict, the Junior Blues played without one of their best doubles players, Reid Osborn. Hayden's doubles team finished fifth, which was higher than Rural's other doubles team, and that preserved the 76-74 team title for Hayden. Rural fell two points short to a very solid Hayden team.

Hedberg refused to use Reid Osborn's absence and a lineup switch he made (playing Murray in doubles instead of singles) as an excuse for losing the title. "We had opportunities, and we played some good matches, and we won some good ones and we lost some close ones," Hedberg recounted. "There's no sin in this except if you don't learn from it, if you don't get better and try to make improvements. Saturday (6A regional competition) is a big day now." Also very positive coach speak. Optimism has its place.

Hayden's coach recognized the significance of his team's accomplishment. "Rural is the pinnacle of tennis programs in our area, so we're always trying to measure up with them," Hayden's James Sandstrom said. "They've got a great program, and Coach Hedberg is a great coach. You always know you're going to get his best shot, so any time that we can do something with them and have a good result, that's good for us."

Regionals came up and, apparently, Rural did learn from their league loss. Murray ended up taking second in singles, and Tanner Driggers took third qualifying for state. In doubles, the team of Osborn and Osborn won the championship, and Garland and Beard placed third. That added up to a 23-18 team title defeating second-place Manhattan. This regional title kept a very impressive streak of regional titles going—fifteen straight years as regional champs.

"It's not been a good two years talking about streaks, so I'm going to forget about that," Hedberg stated. "It's a good regional and very competitive. Manhattan is a good team, and I'm really glad to finish ahead of them because I respect them. I'm very proud of the Osborns. We didn't have Reid for league, and I didn't know how he would react, and the Manhattan team has improved so much over the year, so I was really thrilled with their (Osborn and Osborn) win." The other doubles team of Beard and Garland lost to their teammates in the semifinals and came back to claim third place.

Early, at the state tournament, the Osborn brothers' team fell into the consolation side of the bracket but fought back to claim ninth place and a medal. In the two years of the brothers competing together, they put together a 46-11 record. "I think we had a great season together," Reid the senior said about him and his sophomore brother. "It was great always being together and knowing each other's thoughts and plays."

2015—REPEAT CITY CHAMPIONSHIP FOR TWO STRAIGHT: A NEW STREAK

In their first match of the season, Rural got smacked 3-1 in a dual with Manhattan. This must have awakened their competitive juices because they bounced back in a quadrangular that pitted them against Lawrence, Seaman and Topeka West and swept all four events against each school.

Hedberg told Capital-Journal sportswriter Rick Peterson, "We got punched in the mouth yesterday by Manhattan which has a genuinely good team, and I could tell the boys were anxious to get out here," Hedberg commented. "The conversation we had yesterday was that there's no sin in losing to good teams and good players, but what do you do with it? We didn't play as well as we can (against Manhattan), but we might not have won if we'd done it, so we've got to get better. Today the boys definitely played smarter, and we have to play smart. If we don't play smart, we're not very good."

Freshman Max Cassidy and junior Jordan Lind went 3-0 on the day in singles competition. Senior Kyle Beard teamed with junior Nathan Osborn to go 3-0 in number one doubles. Senior Brendan Garland and junior Tanner Driggers won their first two doubles matches in the number two doubles event, and they were replaced in the third match by the team of senior Liam Weingarten and Driggers, who also won their only match in number two doubles for the team sweep.

At the city event, only the number one singles event escaped them and, even there, freshman Cassidy did himself well by reaching the championship match. But four time city champion Hunter from Hayden captured an 8-1 anticipated victory, sealing the fact he was the best individual player in the city that year.

In capturing the other three events, Rural boys won their twenty-third team title out of twenty-four years. Lind came through in number two singles, downing a Topeka High singles player 8-3. The sweep of the two doubles events gave Rural a 30-19 winning margin over Seaman. Beard and Osborn stayed consistently good, winning the number one doubles event while their doubles teammates Garland and Driggers won in the number two doubles competition.

Kyle Beard and Brenden Garland told Rick Peterson, Capital-Journal sportswriter, that winning the city title is a goal for any player who puts on a Rural uniform and wields a tennis racket.

"It's (city event) like the closest to home, and it's the biggest deal, and we've won it the most out of any of them (other city schools), so it's just kind of good to keep that tradition going," Beard said.

Garland agreed. "We knew that a lot of teams were going to be tough today, and we knew we just had to come out and play our best tennis," he said. "If we did that, we felt pretty good about our chances to come away with a win."

Manhattan seemed to be the Junior Blues' nemesis this season as they also outdistanced them in the Centennial League event, edging Rural 82-80 in a closely-contested event. The doubles teams fared pretty well in this event. Garland and Driggers finished second place while their teammates Osborn and Beard took third place. Max Cassidy rounded out the scoring with a fourth-place finish in singles from Cassidy.

One thing about Coach Hedberg, he's level-headed and pragmatic when he reflects on a tournament. "(Manhattan is) better, and they showed it today. They beat us two out of the three matches in singles, and they beat us in the finals of doubles. They're just a little better team than we are. It's reality," Hedberg told the Capital-Journal. But he was pleased with the way his team fought and clawed. "We played well today," he said, "I was very happy with how we played in the city tournament, and I'm happy with how we played overall today."

Since a regional finish qualifies a team for the state tournament, it would be the event where you hope you would be able to play your best tennis. The Junior Blues played really good tennis at regionals which allowed the Junior Blues to qualify their whole team for the state event a week later.

Washburn Rural made a good showing at the state event finishing eighth place among a very good field of teams. Manhattan finished fifth behind four Kansas City schools. Beard and Osborn finished eighth in doubles, and their teammates Driggers and Garland finished tenth.

2016—TEAM FOUGHT COMPETITION AND ILLNESS FOR STATE TROPHY

While Hayden had continued to march out the best individual player in the city for the previous three seasons—senior Tommy Hunter—Washburn Rural continued its team dominance by winning their twenty-fourth city team title in the last twenty-five years. This was the third win in a row for some of the Rural players. The only interruption to the string was a 2013 team title Hayden earned.

While Hunter shined in singles, Rural's senior Nathan Osborn captured third place in number one singles, while teammate Max Cassidy won the number two singles event.

The doubles competition was a sweep for Rural with the number one doubles team of Ian Clifton and Tanner Driggers taking the number one doubles competition. Their teammates Jordan Lind and Devin Wright teamed up to win the number two doubles, helping lead the Junior Blues to a seven-point team victory, outdistancing Hayden 29-22 for the city event championship.

Coach Hedberg told the Capital-Journal sportswriter Rick Peterson, "We played well today." Hedberg commented, "I've been real pleased with this team overall since the school year started. They're working and the kids right below them in the ladder are working hard, and I think they've kind of got us headed in the right direction. I was real pleased with the result. I thought the boys overall played real well. Honestly, if your goal is to compete at the highest level at the state tournament, which is our goal, you really have to win your city meet. You have to be one of the best tams in your town, if not the best team in town, and it's been a goal a long time for us." Yeah, about twenty-five years worth of expecting that.

You never make excuses, but the fact going into the Centennial League championship event was that three of the top six Rural tennis players were missing the event with the flu. Osborn, Driggers and Wright all were too ill to play. Compound this with the fact that several of Rural's junior varsity players already had played in their allowable two all-day events. Hedberg said it was his first time in thirty-six years of coaching high school tennis he had to scratch even ONE player on the day of the meet, let alone three. But Hedberg assured the disappointed three players that the upcoming regional the following Saturday was much more important for them to get well for.

Originally thought to be a contender against Manhattan, the Junior Blues slipped to fifth place as a team.

At the league meet, Rural was led by Cassidy's third place in singles. Rural's duo of Clifton and Lind ended up playing Hayden's Federico and Sandstrom for third place, and Clifton began feeling ill too, so that doubles team retired before finishing.

On Saturday, with a full complement of players, Rural turned the table on Manhattan beating them 20-18 in the regional event. More importantly, Rural got a third and fourth-place finish in singles when Osborn defeated teammate Cassidy who defaulted the match due to an injury. Rural got a second and third from doubles teams Driggers and Clifton, who finished just ahead of Wright and Lind.

Sophomore Cassidy took an 18-7 singles record to the state tournament accompanied by senior Osborn who sported a 16-1 record in singles. The doubles team of sophomore Clifton and senior Driggers sported an 11-2 record, and their other doubles team of seniors Lind and Wright entered the event with a 12-6 record as a duo.

Cassidy placed seventh at the state tournament after winning three matches on the backside after a second-round loss. "My goal was to medal this tournament, and I did better than just that by getting seventh. I was pretty happy with my performance," Cassidy told Capital-Journal sportswriter Brent Maycock.

Rural had three state placers overall, adding Osborn's eighth-place finish in singles. The duo of Driggers and Clifton finished ninth in doubles.

So the Junior Blues added a third-place trophy to their collection of hardware—their highest team finish at state since 2011. Rural won a tie-breaker with league rival Manhattan. Cassidy said, "I thought it was a great performance by us as a team. We did about all we could ask for."

2017—RETURNS ONLY ONE FROM TOP SIX PLAYERS A SEASON AGO

The previous season, that version of the Junior Blues boys tennis team won city, regionals and finished a very solid third place at the 6A tournament. But that meant very little for the upcoming season when only one out of the top six returned. That might have weighed heavily on a tennis coach, but Hedberg put a positive spin on it when he submitted his preseason capsule to the Capital-Journal newspaper saying, "We have a deep roster but return only one starter off of last year's third-place (at state) team. A key for us will be to develop solid doubles teams that are competitive with the other good teams in our league."

Junior Max Cassidy, who had been sidelined with a strained adductor since February, came back with a vengeance. As a sophomore the year before, Cassidy had won the number two singles event. In 2017, he capped his return from injury with a number one singles championship. The injury, a result of an overhead smash that he was attempting, left him uncertain whether he could play that season. He wrapped the injury and took the singles over a Topeka High player 8-3. Cassidy's singles teammate, freshman Jacek Holroyd, won the number two singles event. Rural also got a win in the number two doubles event from juniors Jesus Ramirez and Andrew Stueve, while the number one doubles team of senior Kyle Peter and junior Landon

Schmidt finished third in number one doubles. Rural needed the depth to be able to earn the team win over Topeka West 29-23.

Hedberg told Capital-Journal sportswriter Rick Peterson that, "I'm real proud of all these guys. They've given me great effort." It was the Junior Blues boys' twenty-fifth city team championship in twenty-six years.

Manhattan set out to defend its 2016 Centennial League team title and did just that, finishing with 84 points while Topeka West finished a distant second with 75. Rural was one point behind West with 74 for third place. Cassidy and Holyrod finished third and fourth in singles. Rural's Schmidt and Peter finished fifth in doubles to round out the team scoring for Rural.

At the regional meet, Topeka High's Clifton continued his singles success over the Rural singles players that season. Cassidy battled hard 6-1, 6-4 for a second-place finish. Cassidy was the city champion. Clifton, the league and regional champion. Both Cassidy and Holroyd qualified for state after Holyrod placed fourth at regional. The doubles team of Schmidt and Peter claimed the regional doubles championship, which helped Rural to its second regional championship in those last two years.

At the 6A state, Cassidy finished ninth for the Junior Blues, capping a seventh-place team finish.

2018—RETURNS EXPERIENCE AND INTELLIGENCE: A GOOD COMBO

The season before, Washburn Rural had faced a stiff Centennial League challenge but managed to capture the city title and their regional title and finished seventh as a team at the state tournament. And they had some of the more solid returners back again.

Hedberg told the Capital-Journal, which profiled preseason for all city schools, "We have a strong core group but face many challenges. Our doubles lineups are still coming together, and we have some injury issues that are yet to be completely resolved. It is a very smart group overall, and we are trying to integrate that intelligence onto the tennis court."

If there's something other than tennis skill that Hedberg is a good judge of it might be intelligence. He teaches advanced placement social studies classes. Applying intelligence to their tennis game proved to be a positive for Rural.

Last year, Rural had won the city title capturing three championships in four events and outscoring Topeka West 29-23. It was the twenty-fifth city title in twenty-six years. The tennis players weren't even born for about eight of the twelve first years of that streak.

With the same two singles champions from the previous year back, they won the number one and number two singles—again! Senior Max Cassidy won number one, and sophomore Jacek Holyrod captured the number two singles again. In 2018, Hayden swept the doubles titles to finish second 27-23. Hedberg switched the duo of Cassidy and Holroyd from doubles to singles for this match. That move paid off. Junior Will Baker and senior Landon Schmidt finished third in number one doubles while their teammates of sophomore Turner Seals and senior Andrew Stueve finished second in number two doubles.

"I think the boys played well," Hedberg told Capital-Journal sportswriter Rick Peterson. "We knew coming in that Hayden was a threat, and sticking (Max and Jacek) out there in singles we felt was a chance to maximize our points, and I think they played well. They looked a little rusty at times, but they played really well, and I was pleased with the guys that were playing doubles and what they were able to accomplish." There is a bit of coaching strategy to employ in high school tennis.

"This (city championship) is something that, once we get to it and if you're able to win and keep it going, they always feel good about it," Hedberg said. Cassidy, who defeated a Seaman singles player 8-1 in the championship match, agreed with Coach. "You don't want to be the team that loses it (the streak)," Cassidy echoed. "You want to keep the tradition going, and just being able to call yourself the best in the city is a nice honor."

Cassidy's switch to doubles was also one of the injury situations the Junior Blues was dealing with. He was sidelined a couple of months with an ankle injury. Doubles is a little less stress on the ankle, but he was happy to get back to the singles. Especially since he won the city singles last season.

At the Centennial League event, two of the teams not from Topeka—Manhattan and Emporia—were able to shove Washburn Rural to third place as a team. Cassidy and his playing partner Holyrod moved back to doubles and, in the championship match of doubles competition, they were leading 6-2, 4-0 over Hayden's perennial powerhouse duo of Fredirico and Sandstrom. The Hayden duo fought back to win six straight and prevailed 8-6, leaving the Junior Blues with a second-place doubles finish. Stueve was able to finish fifth place in singles. Manhattan finished with the top two places in singles to help them score 88 points. Emporia had two strong doubles teams to score 74, outscoring Rural who had 72 for a third-place finish.

At the 6A regional event, Cassidy and Holyrod won the doubles title and qualified for the 6A state event. The doubles team of Baker and Schmidt finished fifth in doubles and qualified for state also. Stueve would join the two doubles teams at state, finishing fifth in singles.

At the state meet Cassidy saw their hopes for a doubles championship dashed with a hard fought quarterfinal loss to a very good Blue Valley Northwest tandem. Baker and Schmidt lost their first doubles match but won the remainder on the day to also reach the consolation side of the bracket. Cassidy and Holyrod finished sixth. Schmidt and Baker finished twelfth.

2019—UNFORESEEN LAST YEAR OF HIGH SCHOOL TENNIS FOR SENIORS AND JUNIORS

Little did this team know that for this year's juniors on the team it would end up being their last year of high school tennis. A year later, the season came to a screeching halt just as it had begun due to a nationwide pandemic and a governor's mandate to shut down attendance at schools for the spring of 2020. This year's juniors would not have a senior season. In the 2019 season, Rural had ten juniors and seniors with an experienced team set to come back. Hedberg's newspaper outlook said, "We have a very deep team one through twenty, and a very good freshman class with great potential."

Washburn Rural annually hosts what Coach Hedberg calls *The Too Big Invitational*. No team scores are recorded. It typically has three singles events. With it being an early season meet, it enables coaches to have an opportunity to see what their three best singles players can do in competition.

Junior Dalton Delaye won the number two singles event and defeated Duffy from Seaman 8-2. He also finished ahead of consolation match schools Gardner-

Edgerton and Manhattan. The deep Rural team entered three entries in the number three singles. Senior Loren Labatos-Dick played a Manhattan player in the finals of that event and finished second. Closely following behind Labatos-Dick in the consolation match were two more Rural players. Rundel defeated his teammate Rubisoff. Rubisoff had to default as a result of an injury. So singles players for Rural on this day showed some depth minus a clearcut number one player.

Rural was shut out of the doubles competition, but some of these singles players likely would fill Rural's doubles teams this season.

In the WR Quadrangular with Rural hosting Lawrence, Seaman and Topeka West. Junior Jacekk Holroyd went 3-0 and captured the number two singles event. Senior Manny Aguirre and his junior partner Turner Seals went 3-0 and won the number one doubles event. Seniors Will Baker and Grant Brooke took the title in the number two doubles event.

Rural bounced back from a one-point team loss to Manhattan from the event the day before. The inclement weather caused spring sports to get off to a slow start. Hedberg said, "We had a lot of nerves yesterday. It was much better today. We had much better play out of our doubles teams. They just seemed a lot more relaxed and focused." Commenting on the weather, Hedberg said, "We needed to get these two meets in and get something going here."

It was business as usual for Washburn Rural at the annual city meet. In the previous twenty-eight years, the Junior Blues claimed twenty-seven team titles. That's stingy. That's consistency. The city title and trophy stayed in Rural's "house" this year, but it was anything but easy as it became a three-way battle between Rural, Hayden and Seaman. In fact only three team points separated the schools. Rural 26, Hayden 23, and Seaman 23. The result of just one match could have made a difference in who won the team championship that year. Rural's Baker and Brooke took the number two doubles title with an 8-6 win over a Topeka West duo. The Junior Blues also got much-needed points from number one singles when freshman Mason Thieu finished second. The number one doubles team of Aguirre and Seals took a fourth-place finish which was important for their team score total.

Of the balance of that year's city event, Hedberg said, "I think we could wind it up and play tomorrow, and somebody else would win. We all (Hayden and Seaman) have strengths and we all have weaknesses, and it's just how they fit together. I was real happy with my singles players' effort, and we're going to continue to get better in doubles, but we're running out of time."

Washburn Rural took second that season at the Centennial League championship. Thieu took third in singles, and Holroyd finished sixth in singles. Seals and Aguirre also finished sixth in doubles which led Rural to 63 team points well short of league champion Manhattan's 77 points. Manhattan fielded an excellent team this year.

At the 6A regional event, Manhattan once again out-distanced the Junior Blues as a team 23-17. Both Centennial League schools qualified all six of their tennis players for the state event. Rural qualified 21-9 Thieu (second place) and 20-9 Holroyd (sixth place) in singles. The doubles teams of Aguirre and Seals 17-13 and Baker and Brooke 15-10 finished second place and fifth place respectfully.

At the 6A state tournament Rural had a tough first day with only one entry making it to Saturday's play. Freshman Mason Thieu had an opening round bye, lost his second match, but came back with a pair of wins to advance to the consolation matches with a chance to medal. And medal he did, finishing a fine freshman season earning a ninth-place state medal.

HEDBERG REFLECTS ON HIS LAST FULL DECADE OF TENNIS 2010-2019

Something noteworthy about the 2010 season would largely go unnoticed by most. The 2010 team did not win the state tournament, but they were the only team to beat Blue Valley North in a dual match during the four-year period that phenom Jack Socks played there. "We beat them 5-4 at their place with freshman Simon Beatty winning both his singles and doubles matches," Hedberg remembers. He predicted, "Had Simon not broken his leg, I am convinced we would have won the state meet." Off of that team, he mentioned that Conner Edwards and Daniel de Zamacoma played tennis at UMKC, Bobby Florence and Jake Long at Washburn University, and Max Cooper joined Bronson Brassel at William Jewell. Hedberg said, "They were truly a great team."

2020—THE SEASON THAT WASN'T

At 5:30 p.m. on Friday, March 13th, a news conference was held in Topeka. Topeka's mayor at the time, Michelle De La Isla, Shawnee County Health Department Director Linda Ochs, and Shawnee County health officer Gianfranco Pezzino responded to the nation's coronavirus pandemic. All Topeka and county schools had gone on spring break and would be returning from various parts of the state, other states and possibly other countries. So the initial move was made to shut down schools and activities for two weeks. The NCAA response likely had a profound effect on what state high school associations did too.

As a result of the precautionary move by the county, The Kansas State High School Activities Association (KSHSAA) shut down the 2019-2020 basketball state tournament, which had already begun. The NCAA previously had shut down all their spring championships that were to occur in the next two weeks. A premature end to March Madness. Subsequently, the NCAA also shut down all spring sports and activities for the remainder of the school year. KSHSAA was closely watching their response.

On Tuesday, March 17, Governor Laura Kelly, working closely with the state's education commissioner Randy Watson, announced all K-12 school districts would remain closed for the remainder of the school year.

A day later, KSHSAA canceled all high school activities, festivals, competitions, etc., through May 29th, citing the governor's action as the deciding factor in

KSHSAA's decision.

Bill Faflick, a former high school athletic director, now the KSHSAA executive director in 2020, issued this statement to the Capital-Journal. "It's never easy to have opportunities not afforded to kids that have been looking forward to them." I previously had worked with Faflick and got to know him when I was athletic director at Washburn Rural. I can assure you, he sincerely felt this way and felt badly for the numerous Kansas student-participants who wanted to be involved in activities. The Association spent the entire day following Governor Kelly's order exploring all alternatives. For the sake of health and safety, this tough decision was made.

There would be a hole in the historical records for Kansas high schools. There would be no city, league, regional nor state competition for boys tennis. For those seniors of 2020, the opportunity would never present itself again. They were simply done—prematurely and tragically—with their high school careers. But other priorities took precedence, and it was hard to argue with the decisions.

It's why, as coaches, we now encourage and remind our participants often that they are not guaranteed another game, another season. It's more real to them now. It's more than just injuries and losses that can cut a season short.

It was not an easy decision to make, nor was it an easy decision to swallow for the teenagers and coaches who eagerly anticipated their seasons like always. The decision was met with both support and dissension, but the intention of the moves were made in the best interest of health and safety. That's pretty hard to argue with. Time would tell if that was the best move, but regardless of opinion, the 2020 spring season would never occur. Nor would there be a basketball champion crowned for the 2019-2020 season. And that was even harder to swallow since the teams had already earned their way to the state tournament.

2021 BOYS SEASON— RURAL LOOKS TO CONTINUE CITY AND LEAGUE STREAKS

Coming off a season where they placed ninth at state in 2019, but with a season of no play because of coronavirus, there were no players returning from that 2019 group.

The preseason capsule in the local paper identified juniors Kyler Knudtson and Nick Luetje as most likely candidates for singles players. They identified a probable doubles team of senior Aryamann Zutshi and senior Jiyoon Park.

However, in the first quadrangular event opening the season, Zutshi played number one singles and won one out of three of his matches—defeating a Lawrence number one player 8-0 but falling to Seaman and Topeka West's number one singles players. Newcomer Von Lintnel competed in the number two singles event, sweeping all three schools—Lawrence, Seaman and Topeka West—to finish 3-0. Luetje teamed with newcomer Mason Casebeer in number one doubles and defeated Seaman and West but dropped their match against Lawrence to finish the day 2-1. Park and Jack Kramer teamed for the number two doubles and swept all three schools finishing 3-0.

In the large ten-team invitational at Topeka West, Washburn Rural narrowly claimed second-place, one point behind Kansas City Christian school 72-71. Zutshi took third in singles as his teammate Von Lintel finished fifth. Luetje and Casebeer finished ninth in doubles.

In the city event, Topeka West made history with their first ever city title, narrowly defeating Washburn Rural by a point, 28-27. Rural's string of successes at the city meet to this point had seen them win twenty-seven out of the last twenty-eight years—the only interruption up to this point being Hayden's win in 2013. And the 2020 season that never occurred.

West's coach Kurt Davids paid a great tribute to Washburn Rural after the city meet, saying, "They've (Rural) been the king pins. We've been competitive consistently, but it's nice to finally get to the top."

Individually, Knudtson finished third in number one singles while his teammate Zutshi took first in the number two singles event. Luetje and Casebeer finished second in number one doubles while their teammates Park and Zach Willingham captured the number two doubles title.

A highlight this season was that Rural qualified their entire team for state, finishing second at regionals. Manhattan took the regional team title 24 to 18. Teammates Knudtson and Zutshi met in the third-place match, and Knudtson won third as Zutshi failed to finish the match but secured fourth place. Casebeer and Luetje finished second in doubles to a Manhattan team 6-2, 6-2. Their teammates, Park and Willingham, finished fifth-place in doubles, downing the Derby duo in a close match 6-4, 7-6 (12-10).

Kyler Knudtson finished eleventh at the 6A state meet in singles. He finished the year with an 18-10 record, finishing first at city, fourth at league, third at regionals. Aryamann Zutshi won a match at state and finished the season with a 21-13 record. He won the city singles title and place fourth at regionals.

The doubles team of Mason Casebeer and Nick Luetje posted a twelfth-place finish at the state meet and finished the season with a 24-14 record. They were runner-up finishers at city and regionals. Jiyon Park and Zach Willingham posted a 20-11 record as a doubles team. They won the city meet.

HEDBERG ANNOUNCED SPRING 2022 SEASON WOULD BE HIS LAST

If a coach knew that they were going to hang it up at season's end, you'd think they would want that to be one of their greatest seasons. A season of championships. I'm certain Hedberg would have welcomed that, but in his preseason outlook in a Top Sport News article by Rick Peterson, Hedberg opted for this. "This is a great bunch of boys, and they're just fun to be around, and they have fun playing tennis. They're great as a group." What, no bold prediction? No *let's go hang another set of banners*? Hedberg's joy centered around the fun and the team chemistry this last bunch possessed. His expectations were reasonable and simple, just like the way he had coached for all those forty-plus seasons.

In 2022, there were some interesting stories associated with some of his players. His number two doubles team of Zach Willingham and Jiyoon Park were a very good high school doubles team, but they were excellent in another extracurricular activity—debate. In fact, so excellent they became the first Kansas public high school debate team to win the National Debate Coaches Association national championship. That was important to Hedberg as well.

In tennis the previous year, the duo captured the city championship for number two doubles event and qualified for state. While they were certainly quality tennis players, the sport served them both as a way to have fun and blow off some steam from the rigors of debate.

Another player, senior Mason Thieu, was an immediate tennis standout for the Junior Blues. As a freshman, he earned a state medal with a ninth-place singles finish at the state event. After losing his sophomore season of 2020 to Covid, he made a move to Florida to attend a tennis academy in hopes to attract some interest from Division One collegiate programs. The move paid off, but not in the way he originally planned.

What he found was that he was, perhaps, getting a little burnt out. He took a step back to focus more on simply enjoying playing tennis. It worked, and he looked forward to simply getting back that love for the game during the 2022 season. Hedberg would appreciate that as well.

In Hedberg's final city tournament, Washburn Rural and Topeka West were co-champions as they tied for the team title 28-28. Hedberg told TopSports.news that he and West's coach, Kurt David, "were talking last night, and we figured out we had three options. One of us was going to win by one point or we were going to tie."

Rural claimed both singles titles with Thieu taking an 8-2 win over West. Mason Casebeer took an 8-1 win over a West player. West turned the tables in doubles, winning both number one and number two doubles events. Kyler Knudtson and partner Nick Luetje took second in number one doubles. Jiyoon Park and Zach Willinham took second in number two doubles.

Thieu told Peterson of TopSports.news, "I wasn't playing too well, but I got it done, and that's what's important."

Washburn Rural closed out the regular season with both the Centennial League championship and a regional championship.

IN HIS SECOND YEAR, HEDBERG ALSO TAKES OVER THE GIRLS PROGRAM 1992–FIRST SEASON COACHING GIRLS AT WASHBURN RURAL

As fate would have it, long-time tennis coach Bob Gladfelter, who had success both at Topeka West and at Washburn Rural, was prepared to take over the athletic director duties at Rural and saw a capable replacement for himself in Kevin Hedberg.

In the fall of 1990, Gladfelter's team won the first state championship in 5A. Three years later Hedberg got number two in 1993. Rural took second at the state championship in 1986 and 1991 under Gladfelter. Hedberg's teams were runners up in 1992 and 2006.

Rural girls finished third place under Hedberg in 1994, 2002, 2003, 2008, 2010, 2011, 2012 and 2013. They were fourth as a team in 2017.

The individual state champions had been the 1994 doubles team of Megan McBride and Jenny Van Vlack, and in 2012, Madeline Hill won the state singles championship.

Danielle Knipp was named four times to the All-State team from 1990 to 1993. Sheri Olivier was named All-State in 2005 and 2006. Taylor Smith, Gwen Shepler and Mackenzie Hill were named to the 2010 All-State team. Madeline Hill was named All-State all four years 2011-2014.

In the 1980s Washburn Rural girls won regional championships between the years of 1981 and 1986. Gladfelter's team also won regionals in 1990 and 1991.

State placers in the 1980s were Jennifer Pasley and Erica Anderson, third in doubles (1981). Sarah Craig and Reina Roberts were fourth in doubles (1982). Lisa Schmoller was fifth in singles (1985). Michelle Knipp was second in singles (1986) and Lisa Schmoller and Paige Evans placed third in doubles (1986). Michelle Knipp also placed second in singles (1987). These were all state placers in the state's classification by enrollment of 5A.

For the school year 1990-91, Washburn Rural's enrollment had grown to a level that placed them in 6A. They were one of the TOP schools for enrollment in the state of Kansas. Danielle Knipp was third in singles, and Heather Dobbs and Marie Gruffy third in doubles (1990). Danielle Knipp was second in singles, and Anne Wiksten and Megan McBride fourth in doubles (1991). Danielle Knipp was second in singles, Megan McBride and Jenny VanVlack fourth in doubles, and Colleen Pendley and Kelly Roberts were fifth in doubles (1992). Danielle Knipp was second in singles, Megan McBride and and Jenny VanVlack second in doubles, and Colleen Pendley and Kelly Roberts fourth in doubles (1993). Megan McBride and Jenny VanVlack were champions in doubles (1994). Cheryl Catron and Michelle Hollins were fourth in doubles (1997). Kassie Baxter and Whitney Hamilton were third in doubles (2002). Sheri Olivier was fourth in singles (2005), and Olivier also placed second in singles (2006). Mackenzie Hill and Gwen Shepler were fourth in doubles (2010). Madeline Hill was fourth in singles in 2011 and went on to finish first in

2012. She finished fourth in singles (2013) and second in 2014.

In addition, the Rural girls dominated the Centennial League, winning every year for that decade (ten straight) and also in 1990 and 1991. In fact, Rural girls won sixteen straight years (1980 through 1995). From 2001 through 2021, they ONLY failed to win the League championship four of those years.

And they began a string of city championships in 1990. They won five straight from 1990 through 1994. They began another string in 2003, winning all but two city titles to date in 2021.

Quite an impressive history as Hedberg finished his thirtieth year coaching at Rural in 2021, and still he and the team were going strong and always in the running.

1992–HEDBERG'S INAUGURAL GIRLS' SEASON AT RURAL

Washburn Rural went into the Topeka City championship in late September as the favorite. They brought with them a 54-4 record. Hedberg took nothing for granted, even though the Junior Blues advanced to all the final matches. But Hedberg knew a split would create a tie with Topeka West. So Rural needed to win at least three of the four finals. They captured all four and defeated West 32-24.

Despite coming off of a shoulder injury in the summer, Danielle Knipp captured the number one singles championship, defeating West's Meg Griffin 9-1.

Rural's only senior, Laura Hill, climbed to a 17-1 record, winning number two singles over Hock 9-3. Both doubles teams won. Megan McBride and Jenie VanVleck defeated Humphrey and Congrove 9-4. Colleen Pendley and Kelly Roberts defeated Sharp and Polly 9-5.

Hedberg was very wary of Topeka West coached by Corey Wilson. Hedberg said before the final matches, "I've seen Corey's kids play awfully well, so those are tough match-ups. Virtually every time we run into West at a tournament, Corey gets the most out of his kids."

Wilson was pleased with his team's efforts. "Washburn Rural has been a tough team for us; they're a great team. I'm real pleased," Wilson told sportswriter Kevin Haskin, "though with the way we played. I think we're getting to be a step closer to where I want us to be. I'm not at all disappointed." I had the privilege of attending college—Washburn—with Corey Wilson. Wilson is a class act.

Washburn Rural, coming off their Centennial League title, added a Regional title to their trophy case, and then it was on to state with a full team representing the Junior Blues. Rural had won state in 1990 and finished second in 1991, so expectations were high going into the tournament.

Hedberg told Kevin Haskin, sportswriter for the Capital-Journal, "Everybody knows we're loaded and we have a very good team, but you still have to go out and play. There are some good teams out there, and we'll have to play well to beat them."

Washburn Rural ended up two points behind eventual champion Shawnee Mission East. There were factors and variables for the finish, but no excuses from Rural. Knipp was battling a knee injury and completed a three-and-a-half hour marathon semifinal match only to turn around and play twenty minutes later in the final match—a match that she had to win to affect the team title. If the Shawnee Mission East player had lost her third-place match, that could have caused a tie, which Rural would have won due to a scoring component that favors the team with the most players. Rural had all six. But it was just not meant to be.

Years later, Hedberg mentioned to me that a decision at the coach's seeding meeting very likely cost Rural the championship. A girl from Shawnee Mission East who was seeded high at the meeting took eighth place without a win.

Hedberg looked for the good in the experience, though. He told Capital-Journal reporter Tony Jimenez, "She (Knipp) just ran out of gas. I don't feel bad or disappointed about how she and we did as a team. She did everything that she could have."

1993—CAN IT GET BETTER THAN RUNNER UP? WELL, ONE CAN DREAM (TEAM)

If, in your first year as the head coach ('92), your team captures the city championship, the league championship, the regional championship and finishes second at the 6A State tournament, it's hard to improve upon that. But season number two looked awfully good on the front side, especially if your number-one player is senior Danielle Knipp who, to date, had compiled an 85-5 record and been a state placer all of her three previous years.

In an August 31st preseason article in the Topeka Capital-Journal, sportswriter Kevin Haskin pointed out an interesting fact. Washburn Rural captured the state crown in 1990, then Shawnee Mission East won in both 1991 and 1992. What Haskin pointed to was that the Washburn Rural point total at the tournaments had been on a steady climb.

They scored 24 points in 1990 to win the title, then scored 28 in 1991 to be runner-up, and scored a whopping 33 in 1992, also runner-up. So Rural hadn't slipped as a team regarding scoring points. Knipp had captured the city, league and regional titles in each of her three tennis seasons. She had two third-place finishes in singles at state and was second as a junior. Knipp was receiving recruiting attention from Florida State, Notre Dame, and Kansas among other major colleges seeking her talents.

But Hedberg also had four other state qualifiers returning for the upcoming season—seniors Colleen Pendley and Kelley Roberts, and juniors Megan McBride and Jenie Van Vlack. McBride and VanVlack placed fourth in 6A doubles the previous fall while Pendley and Roberts placed fifth. Freshman Emily Lee was projected to move into the sixth spot for the girls team.

Haskin asked Hedberg about the upcoming season, and Hedberg said, "My biggest fear is complacency, which can come from being expected to be good and then not working." Hedberg followed that up with, "But so far, I haven't seen that. And last year, I thought at the state meet some of our girls played their best tennis of the year."

Topeka West, Hayden, and Shawnee Heights returned state-caliber players as well, so the city tournament looked like it would be strong competition. Heights and Hayden would compete with Rural for League. Solid competition during the regular season can be advantageous as you prepare to play the elite players in your state tournament.

In early September, Washburn Rural swept singles and doubles at the Seaman Invitational. Knipp and Lee captured singles wins. Both doubles teams won. Out of six teams, Junction City was the closest competition, but Rural outscored them 28 to 17.

By the time the city championship rolled around, Washburn Rural was on a winning streak like no other. They outscored Topeka West 32 to 23. Shawnee Heights barely nudged Hayden for third place 17 to 16. And for the season, Washburn Rural ran their streak of consecutive matches won to sixty with no defeats thus far in that stretch of competition.

Senior Danielle Knipp capped her four-year sweep of number one singles city championships by defeating Meg Griffin from Topeka West 8-3. The Junior Blues freshman, Emily Lee, fought hard for the number two singles title, outlasting Danielle Carter from Topeka West 9-8 (7-5).

In doubles, Megan McBride and Jenie Van Vlack triumphed at number one team by defeating Hayden twins Morey and Caroline Graham 8-3 in the finals. At number two doubles, Colleen Pendley and Kelley Roberts defeated Heather Farris and Amy Schick of Topeka West 8-1.

Knipp surpassed the 100-win plateau, and Hedberg guesstimated that Roberts and Pendley were pushing eighty wins in their career. So much for Hedberg's concern a month previously about possible complacency. He told sportswriter Haskin in his Topeka-Capital Journal re-cap of the city championship, "That (complacency) was my worry before the season started and really, they've done pretty well." Hedberg also pointed out, "We take everybody seriously, but these kids have enough experience they know to do that."

In early October, they continued their sweep of matches, winning all of them at their own invitational, finishing a 28 to 14 margin over second-place Blue Valley North. Evidently, the cupboard was in the process of reloading, because the Washburn Rural junior varsity captured the city championship as well. There were good young girls in the program developing nicely.

Washburn Rural won their fourteenth consecutive Centennial League title as they prepared for regionals. In an eight-team regional, Washburn Rural more than doubled the points over second-place Manhattan 14 to 6, capturing the team title. Knipp captured the regional singles title, defeating her Wichita Heights opponent 6-0, 6-1. McBride and Van Vlack captured second in doubles, beating their teammates Roberts and Pendley who took third.

In this, the season of 1993, the state tournament began a new format. The Kansas State High School Activities Association member schools voted to have the state tournament go to a two-day format. It was to be on an experimental basis this first year to make a determination about how it went. In tennis, a team can host the state tournament, and it was Washburn Rural who put in a bid to host, so it was to be held at Kossover Tennis Center. Two rounds would be played on Friday, and the semifinals and finals on Saturday.

In an article by Topeka Capital-Journal sportswriter, Kevin Haskin, Hedberg had an opinion about the move to a two-day format. Hedberg told Haskin, "Four two or three-set matches is more than one kid should play." As an example of what that old format could look like, he cited the previous year's tournament challenges faced by Knipp. She had already played six or seven hours of tennis before reaching the state finals in 1992.

"In past years, we've had a lot of kids limping through the finals because of cramping, and there have been some defaults," Hedberg mentioned. A default is when a player can no longer continue competing due to injury or fatigue. Hedberg added, "You don't want to see that kind of a thing especially at the state tournament."

The 1992 singles finalists looked like favorites to meet again. Knipp, runner up in '92, brought a 23-0 record to state. That year's champion, Christie Sim from Shawnee Mission South, was 20-0. The doubles team of McBride and Van Vlack improved to 24-0 after handing their teammates Pendley and Roberts their first loss of the season who themselves brought a 25-1 record to state. Overall, Rural captured ninety-one out of ninety-five matches leading up to state.

Shawnee Mission East, once again, looked like the team to beat in 1993.

Due to inclement weather, day one of the state tournament was moved indoors, and all three of Rural's entrants advanced to the semifinals. The number one singles, along with both doubles teams, would be in the semi-finals. Not only advancing, but Rural captured 38 points on day one, and their biggest challenger for the team title—two-time state champions Shawnee Mission East—scored only 28.

With that deficit, despite two Rural entrants finishing second, the Junior Blues still had more than enough points to capture the 6A team title.

Knipp once again was runner-up to her nemesis Christie Sim, but the duo played possibly their closest matches. Each set found deuce. In fact, Knipp was up 5-3 in the first set before Sim took the next four games.

In Haskin's article in the Capital-Journal, he interviewed the champion Sim, and she had this to say about Knipp. "Danielle does a really good job and hits deep shots on her ground strokes." This caused Sim to rush the net more often. She continued, "I knew I couldn't let her continue to do that or she would have beat me."

Knipp told Haskin, "I played really good at the beginning and then let a few opportunities get by, and she (Sim) played really well."

Knipp mixed soft chips with blazing ground strokes in an effort to win. She said, "The score shows it was close, but each game was close also. One point or two may have determined the match because I think every game went deuce (tied)."

Van Vlack and McBride also carried a 27-0 record into the doubles finals, and they also led early before falling 7-5, 6-1 to Aimee Hites and Laura Brady from Shawnee Mission East. It was the East duos' third straight state title.

Rural's other doubles entry of Pendley and Roberts lost to Hites and Brady in the semifinals before they dropped a 9-4 pro-set match in the third-place match. They finished fourth. As a result, second, second, and fourth provided Rural (38 team points) with a ten-point team win over Shawnee Mission East (28).

After the state championship belonged to Rural, Hedberg told Haskin, "This was my dream team. I could coach for twenty years and not have another one like this. I know they're all disappointed because they didn't win their last matches, but only ONE team won it and we're the team."

There was reflection by the media and others about Danielle Knipp's career. So many tennis players who would enter high school with the knowledge they would finish third at state two years and second for the other two would say, "that's an outstanding career." It was, but being so close makes one think about what could have been. Hedberg, the history guy, summed it up best in Haskin's article. "She may be the best player in Kansas history to have never won a state title." Knipp's fate was more a matter of timing than a reflection of talent. She came through when the tennis players in 6A were very solid. Outstanding in their own right. Dawn Buth of Wichita Southeast and Angie Popek of Shawnee Mission Northwest were the ones to beat her in the semifinals her freshman and sophomore year. And of course, Sim in her junior and senior years, handed her second-place finishes.

Hedberg attributed a significant portion of her career to her focus on team and team success. She could have missed high school practices and hit with bigger, stronger men to improve her game, but she chose to practice every single day and make her teammates stronger. That is a big sacrifice in an individual sport.

McBride was another interesting story. She opted to play dual sports in the fall of her junior year—golf and tennis. She helped the golf team qualify for their state tournament. This kind of selfless chemistry was present for the 1993 team.

Hedberg reflected on finally capturing that elusive state title. "I'd say if we hadn't won it, it would have been a disappointment. To lose it at the very end two years in a row was tough on the girls. I know it bothered me for six months after last season.

But to come back and win it this year is a tribute to the kids—their spirit and their friendship. They have such a feeling for each other."

That feeling for each other was present at the state tournament in 1993 just as it probably was present as their team was inducted into the Washburn Rural Hall of Fame in December of 2021.

As Hedberg reflected on that special team he really wanted to point out that, at that time, Kansas was likely one of the three or four best states in regard to producing quality girls' tennis players. Remember, he had been in Florida and Texas and saw other states. The pecking order was then probably California, Texas and Florida for girls that were nationally ranked. Hedberg attributed a lot of the state's success to great teaching.

All of these variables make Danielle Knipp's accomplishments so special. Hedberg said, "Danielle was a fabulous player. Two-hands on both sides."

"That whole group loved each other and they enjoyed playing. After 1992, we lost one senior, Laura Hill. She graduated. Then came freshman Emily Lee, and those girls took her under their wing and they made her a part of it, and they made her ready to be the team leader in a couple of years."

Hedberg also remembered that Kelly Roberts could take an overhead and pound it. She intimidated a lot of opponents. After taking a couple of hits, opponents backed off a bit. She was a strong athlete, and she threw the discus for the track team. She was a fierce competitor too.

Colleen Pendley was from a tennis family, and she played exceptionally well as an integral part of the championship group.

Megan McBride was a tremendous tennis player who likely could have had a great singles career, but with Jenie Van Vlack, Hedberg knew that they stood the best chance of capturing a doubles championship together. It takes good talent, selfless athletes and a coach who knows how to handle the physical play as well as handle the mental part of the game of tennis that is so important.

At the Hall of Fame ceremony in 2021, Hedberg said, after all those years, he had forgotten, until the content of the book was absorbed, that their margin of victory was nine points. And it really wasn't even that close. A dream season. A dream team.

CHAMPIONSHIP PLAYER REFLECTIONS

Years later, does the championship experience dwindle in importance? Quite the opposite, and with maturity and with life's travels for these women, it seems that adulting garners an even greater appreciation for past accomplishments. High school was a magical time for these women.

Tennis players like Danielle Knipp come a coach's way so infrequently. Knipp and Hedberg established a relationship together long before high school tennis brought them back together. So it was a natural question and a perspective that only a competitor who worked with Hedberg could answer: What makes Hedberg a good tennis coach?

As Knipp reflected, she said, "Boy, this is a tough question." Because of multiple years working on her skills with Hedberg's lessons and coaching, she said, "I knew Kevin well before he was the tennis coach at Washburn Rural, and he was a huge part of over a decade of my life."

She went on to say, "Kevin was a tremendous coach because he is simply an amazing person. Kevin's outlook on life, his storied past, and his love for tennis is what made him amazing." Knipp added the important factor. "There are very few coaches like Kevin; he truly gave his heart to those he coached, and was like a family member to many."

She mentioned that Hedberg had a great perspective about young teenagers saying, "Kevin knew how to balance tennis with all that we had going on with life as well and was there to guide and support us. We were so lucky to have this type of support during such formative high school years. Wouldn't it be amazing if all high school students had this? What a difference that could make."

The majority of successful coaches know how to build relationships and understand that, while tennis is important, relationships trump all else associated with team sports. Knipp commented, "He truly got to know each and every player, regardless of skill level, and was able to coin a nickname that was truly a perfect fit for each player within days of meeting them." Athletes may forget specific sets and points during their high school tennis matches, but they remember the nicknames and the caring and compassion their coaches provide them.

Knipp came from a tennis-playing family, so she had a father and an older sibling to get additional advice and help from. Knipp appreciatively said, "I was lucky to have a dad who coached me as well, which isn't always a desirable situation for some high school coaches, but Kevin embraced having my dad along for the ride." Again, something that endeared Hedberg to not only Danielle, but her family. He was considered a part of the Knipp family.

With time there comes realizations that most have regarding mentors in our lives. Knipp admits, "I often feel like I haven't thanked Kevin enough as he truly was such an important piece of making me who I am today." But Knipp expresses this wish that "most importantly I do hope he knows that he truly made an impact and a difference in thousands and thousands of students' lives. Playing at national and collegiate tennis levels, I came across many coaches and none were like Kevin. Each athlete and each student he's had are so fortunate and truly blessed." From Danielle (Knipp) Ulrich circa 2021.

Can there be any better compliments than those?

Maybe not better, but equally complimentary of her coach, Kelly (Roberts) Lincoln also reflected about her time spent on the Washburn Rural tennis team under Coach Kevin Hedberg. As she looked back on her four-year career at Washburn, she realized what an "important role Hedberg played in my athletic and academic career."

Roberts went on to say, "Coach Hedberg is a legendary coach, teacher and person. He has created a coaching legacy that few can accomplish." Indeed he has. It's a unique and special blend when athletic talent and great coaching collide. Roberts continued, "Coach knew what motivated us individually and as a team. He used that knowledge when talking game plans and strategy." And he did it with a style uniquely Hedberg's. He did it with compassion, purpose, and with a dose of that Hedberg humor that is often times unmatched.

Roberts remembered "one practice the night before a tennis meet. It may have been before the city event or the league tournament. He was going over strategy with Colleen Pendley, my doubles partner, and I. We were asking so many questions like, 'what if they hit it here? What if they don't return the serve cross court? Or what should I do if they both come to the net?" She said that Hedberg could read the anxiety in their voices through their questions. To add some levity and perspective to the questions, Hedberg said something along the lines of "what if an alien came out of the sky and hit a winner down the middle?" Apparently it worked, because Roberts remembers all three laughing. She also realized that she and her partner were just nervous and that there was no possible way to anticipate every move their opponents were going to make. She added, "Hedberg emphasized we had to play OUR game." "Their game" was a pretty good one. Hedberg knew that.

Hedberg created relationships with his players both on and off the court. Roberts says, "Another memory I will forever cherish is when Coach asked me to house-sit for him. I think it was for a weekend, but it may have been for a week. I was so honored that he trusted me to watch his house and dog while he and his wife were gone. I remember being so diligent about cleaning and organizing because I didn't want Coach to be disappointed in my work. It was a great experience for me. One I will never forget."

Roberts told me that she is certain there are plenty of other stories, but it is difficult for her to remember specifics. She did mention an important memory and an important aspect of why Washburn Rural tennis was/is so successful under Hedberg. "I know for a fact, each year our team laughed a lot; we were ornery and had way too much fun." I believe Coach Hedberg would say something similar, except there never can be too much fun when you are doing something you enjoy with the someones you enjoy doing it with. Success can be the icing.

Tragically, Megan McBride (Franz) passed away after a long battle with cancer at the age of 31 in 2009. Megan went on to Kansas University after graduating from Rural and earned her degree in Business Administration in 1999. She was employed as a Sales Executive with Cerner Corporation in 2001. She had married Alex Franz in 2004, and they made their home in Overland Park, Kansas. Megan was an integral part of that great team and their historic 1993 state championship season. Her folks, Tom and Meef McBride, are Megan's parents and longtime residents of Topeka. Megan is missed by many. Gone way too soon.

1994—WHAT WOULD THE YEAR AFTER THE DREAM TEAM BE LIKE?

The team looked slightly different, but the doubles team of Megan McBride and Jenni Van Vlack returned. Although they split up at the League meet—giving McBride a chance to play number one singles in the absence of Danielle Knipp—they would reunite at regionals and state competition.

At the Centennial League meet, McBride won the number one singles, beating a Hayden freshman Libby Brooks 6-0, 6-0. In the Capital-Journal sports article by sportswriter Mark Willett, Hedberg pointed out the obvious. "She would probably have been our number one singles player the last three years, but we had Danielle, so Megan played number one doubles for us."

Knipp took her game to the University of Wisconsin, so McBride added a singles title to her other three doubles championships at the Centennial League meet.

"These were my first number one singles matches of the year. I just needed a break from doubles," McBride told the Capital-Journal.

While McBride was enjoying some singles, Van Vlack teamed with Jennefer Lux to win the number two doubles crown.

The change up was as much for McBride and Van Vlack's mental preparation as it was a ploy to capture the league title, which Rural did, defeating the second-place

Emporia 26 to 19.

Hedberg mentioned that the doubles team of McBride and Van Vlack would be under a lot of pressure as favorites to win the doubles championship at regionals and state. They were second at state in 1993.

At regionals, McBride and Van Vlack won the championship over their teammates Lee and Sanders, running their season record to 25-0, but Topeka West won the team championship by the narrow margin of 14-11.

At the 6A state tournament, McBride and Van Vlack won their doubles championship. To date, they are the ONLY girls state doubles champions in Rural's school history. One more special feat by the remnants of the 1993 state championship team.

1995—GIRLS RUN THEIR STRING OF CENTENNIAL LEAGUE TITLES TO SIXTEEN STRAIGHT

Washburn Rural's tennis team kept their string of league titles, winning their sixteenth in a row. Sixteen straight years. Five consecutive trips to the state tournament.

In the Capital-Journal's outlook for the season, they pointed out that Rural had four returning letterwomen—Jessica Sanders, Emily Lee, Jennifer Lux and Kelly McKenzie.

Also, in the preseason capsule in the Topeka Capital-Journal, Hedberg said he had ten to twelve girls that were good players and "interchangeable."

"I believe we will be competitive and stronger this year," Hedberg mentioned. "I want us to have fun since we've had pressure on us in the past."

If there is a trademark to Kevin Hedberg's tennis recipe, it's *enjoy the ride*. Have fun and enjoy the experiences, value the relationships you can make. Really, when you think about the grand scheme of things, isn't that what high school sports should be about?

Injecting my opinion based on being a patron, a parent of three Washburn Rural athletes, a coach, and an athletic director as well as a school administrator for forty-plus years—if more people had this healthy perspective, there would be more joy and highs associated with high school sports. And club sports as well. So many of these experiences are out of whack because the focus gets shifted to potential scholarships, publicity, championships, etc. I'll step off that soap box, but if you're reading this, please think about it and reflect as a coach, parent or grandparent. Sports are meant to be enjoyable and a positive, developmental learning piece for high schoolers to be able to take advantage of.

In 1995, Washburn Rural won matches and were competitive all year. There would not be a city championship, nor a regional championship, but to capture the sixteenth straight Centennial League title was pretty special. Especially since that string would be broken the next year.

Also, Emily Lee, junior, won the regional singles title.

I guarantee, the experience on the Washburn Rural tennis team was viewed as worthwhile and fun, in part, thanks to Coach Kevin Hedberg and his healthy perspective and the words he inevitably shared with his players along the way.

1996—AN UNUSUAL YEAR INDEED

There would be a city championship, and then it would be another seven years to win the next one. There would be no league championship. (In fact, it was a six-year drought there as well.) Of course, that meant no regional championship in 1996, although, they would win regionals within just ONE year (1997).

High school sports are funny. You may not be a dominant team in your city, in your league, but yet you CAN be good enough to capture a regional championship. Sometimes the combination of schools in the city and the league are tougher challenges than who they put in a regional event.

In the preseason article, the Capital-Journal looked at local tennis. Washburn Rural had Emily Lee, Kelly McKenzie, Jennifer Lux, Becky Stauffer and Cheryl Catron as returning letter winners. As a junior the year before, Lee was 28-7 as a singles regional winner.

The number two doubles team of Stauffer and Catron won the Centennial league title the year before. Hedberg felt with the seniors returning there could be a very good season ahead. Hayden, Topeka High, and Topeka West appeared to be very strong this season.

When it rolled around to the city championship, Rural appeared to be peaking well. According to the Capital-Journal article by sportswriter Brett Goering—a Washburn Rural student at the time and son of the late and former sports editor

Pete Goering—Emily Lee may have played her best match of the year to win the number one singles.

Lee won her match 8-3 against Hayden's Malini Desilva. The other city championship came from the number two doubles team from Rural, Michelle Hollins and Cheryl Catron, as they defeated Topeka High's team of Linsey Roth and Michelle Nantz 8-3.

"We had a good day today. Some kids stepped up and played real well. It always helps a team when their number one singles player can win their event," Hedberg commented. "Emily did her job and played the best I think she's played, and that took a lot of pressure off the other girls." Lee was second as a junior in the previous year's city championship.

Lee said, "I think this is the best I've played this year. Malini is a good player, and when we get together, you usually get to see some pretty good tennis. I've had a problem of keeping the ball in play, so I figured if I could keep the ball in play she would make the mistakes. I just wanted to play consistent and smart and move the ball around."

In the number two singles, Kelly McKenzie finished second, dropping her match to Haydent's Libby Rooks 8-1.

The Topeka High number one doubles champions defeated Rural's Jennifer Lux and Becky Stauffer 8-3, but the second-place points earned by them and McKenzie helped the team total.

Hedberg's Rural team score of 28 was seven better than second place Topeka High's 21, but Hedberg, prior to the meet, had a premonition and voiced it. "I really think this meet was wide open with Topeka High, Hayden and Topeka West. Our girls played very well, and we were very fortunate."

His prediction about the future of Topeka high school tennis proved true. Hedberg said, "The city's changing, and the city meets are going to be much more competitive than they have been. The days of one school dominating are pretty much over, so this is one I'm real happy with."

Centennial League school Emporia High would end the Washburn Rural run of sixteen straight league titles. That's sixteen years, sixteen different senior classes. That kind of league dominance is very rare in any sport.

Emporia won the number one singles and number one doubles to upset the Junior Blues string. They won the team championship by one point—23-22. Catron and Hollins were the only league champions in number two doubles. The other three entries captured second place finishes. It's hard to be disappointed with those results.

Hedberg, ever the one to accept responsibility, said in a Capital-Journal article by sportswriter Brett Goering, "Truthfully, I think I underestimated Emporia." He went on to say, "I have no complaints, the girls played very hard, and I'm as proud of the girls as I've been all year. Emporia just played real well and got the better of us." Hedberg knew how to conduct himself with the media. He was always very gracious and complimented the other schools and their players when they played well.

In the 6A tennis championships, Rural, as a team, finished in fifth place—curiously three points better than Emporia (14-11). Ahead of them were champions Shawnee Mission South who scored 35 points.

Jennifer Lux and Becky Stauffer finished seventh in doubles at the state tournament. Rural earned a couple of ninth-place finishes, one from the doubles team of Cheryl Catron and Michelle Hollins, and one from Emily Lee in singles.

1997—OPTIMISM, THE JUNIOR BLUES THEME

Initially, I could find very little information about the 1997 fall girls tennis season. From the record book, you won't find a city championship, nor a league championship for this season. What you will find is that the Junior Blues fared well in their Wichita Regional, finishing third as a team and qualifying three players for the 6A state tournament. Sheryl Catron and Michelle Hollins finished fourth and advanced after losing to the Emporia doubles team of Pam Putnam and Ashley Mitchell 3-6, 6-4, 7-6, (7-3).

In singles, Erin Underwood also finished fourth place in singles, dropping the consolation match to Emporia's Martha Gaunt 6-3 and 6-0.

As a team, Washburn Rural finished third—one point ahead of Centennial League rival Emporia—by a team score of 5-4. Wichita Southeast and Manhattan finished one and two, both scoring ten team points in the competition.

The state tournament was in Hutchinson in 1997 and, just as they had finished in regionals, the doubles team of Catron and Hollins took fourth place at the state tournament. They became the sixteenth and seventeenth Washburn Rural girls tennis players to place at state.

1998—SEASON OVERVIEW

In an early season tennis match in the fall of 1998, the Washburn Rural girls—by one team point—won their invitational match that included second-place finishers Emporia and Hayden, each with 21 team points. In fourth-place was Shawnee Heights with 20, Wamego in fifth with 13, and Seaman who had 7. Rural had won the match, but by the narrowest of margins with a score of 22. By all indications, the Centennial League looked like a strong tennis league, and the city tennis looked even better.

In fact, at the city event, Rural finished an uncharacteristic fourth place among the field of seven which was indicative of the parity in Topeka girls' tennis in the fall of 1998.

The Junior Blues' strength appeared to be the doubles events early in the season. The doubles team of Erin Underwood and Michelle Hollins defeated the second-place Hayden team. The other doubles team of Amy Lee and Toti Walia finished second to an Emporia doubles team. If either team had slipped, there would have been a different outcome for the team finish at the league event. As it played out, Rural finished second place in the Centennial because of their four good doubles players.

In an interesting twist after a fourth and a second-place finish at city and league, Rural played well at their regional and took third place as a team.

Springing into state with some confidence, Rural placed top ten as a team capturing ninth-place.

1999—MANHATTAN, A BIG OBSTACLE

The 1999 tennis team did not capture the city, league or regional championship. Manhattan was an obstacle.

Rural finished second to Manhattan at regionals by a 14-6 team score margin. Rural also finished second in the league meet.

Erin Underwood finished fourth in singles, losing to third place finisher Stark from Wichita Southeast 6-4, 1-6, 6-4, which qualified her for state.

After capturing second at regionals, the doubles team of Kristin Underwood and Mindi Lewis took third place, defeating a Wichita East doubles team in the consolation match.

Hedberg felt his team competed as well as they could, telling the Capital-Journal sports reporter, "I was a little surprised to get second place as a team, but the kids played well. It was a good day."

At the state tournament, Erin Underwood—the lone Topeka singles qualifier—lost her first match but won her second. The doubles team of Kristin Underwood and Mindi Lewis also dropped their first match, but rebounded to win the second match. On the second day, Underwood and Lewis dropped the seventh-place match to the Topeka High doubles team, and Erin Underwood finished tenth to end the season. Blue Valley North won the team title. Topeka High and Rural were part of a four-way tie for seventh place.

2000—ONE WITHOUT MUCH HEDBERG

Perhaps the most unusual loss of the 2000 fall season was that of Coach Kevin Hedberg. Hedberg missed the majority of the season due to a surgery he underwent. He turned over the coaching role to his assistant, Jim Dinkel.

The girls fought through the adversity well and placed second at the league event and also second at the regional event.

Sophomore Kate Johnson finished her singles season with a 16-13 record and qualified for the state tournament. Akihla Challa, a junior, finished her season 19-9.

Doubles partners, sophomore Hannah Wittmer and junior Katie Owen, finished tenth place at state with a 22-10 record. Juniors Caroline Stauffer and Joanna Carpenter posted fourteen wins and seven losses.

Challa told the yearbook reporter, "The varsity squad had an awesome year. Although we didn't have Coach Hedberg, Coach Dinkel did a good job."

2001– RETURN TO LEAGUE AND REGIONAL CHAMPIONS

The 2001 edition of the girls tennis team won their Centennial League championship and were regional champions as well. Actually, they shared the league title with Emporia, so both schools hung a banner. The Centennial League doesn't break team championship ties. Let both get the recognition deserved. The Junior Blues ended a five-year drought, their last league title coming in 1995. Rural did not, however, win the city title.

At the league meet, Emporia owned the singles matches, winning both championships. Rural did the same in doubles. The tie did not disappoint the Rural coach.

Hedberg told Capital-Journal sportswriter Rick Peterson, "This is good. We were real disappointed after the city meet." Hedberg went on to explain, "We felt like we really didn't play real well (in a second place finish at city) and we wanted to do well today. We'll take half of it and be happy with that."

Katie Owen and Caroline Stauffer provided a doubles championship, as did the team of Kassi Baxter and Whitney Hamilton. Joanna Carpenter finished second in number two singles and Katie Johnson finished third in number one singles to round out the Rural team score that matched Emporia's.

"My three senior girls (Owen, Stauffer and Carpenter) have worked really hard on their tennis, and it's not like it's been easy for them to do." Hedberg appreciated these girls academic focus. "They're all high-achieving kids, and they have a lot of other things they do between debate, newspaper and forensics and all these things, so they did a nice job of dedicating themselves, and it's nice to see them have a good situation."

The culmination of the season saw the Junior Blues win their tennis regional and finish a respectable fourth at the state tournament, boasting three top-ten finishers at state. Baxter and Hamilton defeated a Topeka High tandem in doubles for a seventh-place finish. In singles, Kate Johnson was eighth. The Junior Blues duo of Owen and Stauffer placed tenth as Rural was only one point away from Emporia who finished third.

2002–JOINS TWO PREVIOUS RURAL TEAMS: THIRD PLACE STATE FINISHERS

The Junior Blues ended up with only three returning seniors for the fall of 2002—Kate Johnson, Jessica Wayner and Hannah Wittmer. Juniors Whitney Hamilton, Kassie Baxter, Abby Brownback, Aubrey Hirsch and Kristin Munker also were returning from 2001.

The Topeka Capital-Journal listed three top newcomers—junior Lauren Lohse and freshmen Christine Tomlin and Shannon Underwood.

Those returning were part of the team that shared the Centennial League title with Emporia, captured the regional championship, and finished fourth in the state tournament. Hedberg told the Capital-Journal, "We have a good nucleus and hope to repeat last year's continued improvement. They are a fun bunch to be around and seem to enjoy each other."

The girls did not win the city title—only winning one event and dropping the city title to Topeka High—but they had a score to settle in the Centennial League meet. And settle it they did.

The Junior Blues captured three of the four divisions. The only event they did NOT end up winning was the number one singles. That belonged to DeBlonk of Emporia. She defeated Rural's number one Hannah Wittmer 8-3, but Rural captured the other three events. In the number two singles, Kate Johnson defeated Emporia's Kretsinger 8-2.

Both doubles teams—number one Kassie Baxter and Whitney Hamilton—defeated a Shawnee Heights doubles team 8-6.

Even though the best tennis player may have been from Emporia, the stronger group was by far Rural's. Hedberg supported that notion, telling Capital-Journal sportswriter Rick Peterson, "Emporia's got the best player in our league with Megan DeBlonk, but I was pleased with how we came through." He reflected, "We've needed to do that, and we've been unable to do it in a couple of meets, so it's nice to do it (capture three events)."

The reference included the second-place finish to Topeka High at the recent city meet. "I really didn't mention that. The city meet's past, so you don't dwell on it. You don't want to have it on their mind, other than in a positive way."

Hedberg went on to mention that his team had a regional coming up. He spoke positively about Rural's chances at regionals, saying, "We have a bona fide chance to get several people in, so we just want to get better and play better towards that."

Washburn Rural held a six-point team margin over Emporia when it was over, 26-20. No tie this year. Rural went on to capture the regional tennis title the following Monday, as well.

So, heading into state was a confident bunch of Rural tennis players. Every team would like to finish the last tournament in a higher position than the previous year's efforts, and Rural did. Finishing fourth in 2001, they improved on that. They took home the third-place trophy in 2002. Lawrence Free State and Blue Valley North finished a fierce battle, both with 32 team points. The team title was awarded to Blue Valley North based on a tiebreaker. Washburn Rural earned 23 team points.

The Junior Blues were the only team with four qualifiers and saw all four of those place, led by a third-place finish from the doubles team of Baxter and Hamilton. That duo was involved in the two best matches of the day. In the semifinals, the

Rural duo lost a three-set heartbreaker to Blue Valley North's doubles team 6-1, 2-6, 6-1. Baxter and Hamilton bounced back to defeat an Olathe East tandem by the scores of 7-6 (7-5), 7-6 (7-5) and finished their doubles season with a record of 23-4. At the time, it was the highest placing by a girls' doubles team since 1993's Megan McBride and Jenni VanVlack (2nd at state in doubles).

Hannah Witmer, a fourth-place regional finisher in singles, lost her first state match, then stormed back to win three and finally finished sixth. Kate Johnson finished tenth in singles as did the doubles team of Brownback and Wayner.

The 2002 team joined the teams of 1996 and 2000 as the only Rural third-place state finishers. The 1988 team had won state, and the 1999 team had captured second place.

The season for Hedberg was memorable. He said, "This was a really fun group of girls. This was also the year that I lost my eyesight in my right eye due to an accident that occurred at practice."

2003–JUNIOR BLUES QUALIFY ALL SIX FOR STATE

The girls had had a drought in the city championships, but that would change in 2003. Hedberg and his team thought they were legitimate contenders in 2002, but were edged by Topeka High by a single point.

"Last year was very tough," said Hedberg whose team won their first city championship since 1995. "We had it totally in our control, and it got away from us and the High girls outplayed us down the stretch."

Hedberg knows that you can't always just look at what's on paper before a match. "You line it all out and you know it's possible, but you still have to go play, and we got some good performances today. It was a real good day," Hedberg said.

Freshman Cat Huang captured the number two singles event, defeating Lee from Topeka High 8-2. Number one singles player Whitney Hamilton battled High's Stephanie Johns, dropping an 8-5 match for second place.

Similarly the number one doubles team of Baxter and Brownback finished second to a Topeka West duo, dropping the championship match 8-2, and the number two doubles team of Munker and Hirsch won their event with an 8-2 win over the Topeka West duo.

Rural similarly won their Centennial League title for the third year in a row as they tuned up for their regionals.

Rain in Topeka couldn't dampen the day for Washburn Rural at the regional meet. The meet was moved from outdoors at Kossover to indoors at Topeka

Country Club at the halfway mark. Washburn Rural dominated singles with first and second-place finishes from Hamilton and Huang. Doubles did the same when Hirsch and Munker defeated their teammates Baxter and Brownback. The 18 team points far out-distanced the second place Junction City 18-6.

Hedberg elatedly told Capital-Journal sportswriter Rick Peterson, "This is our second year in a row (qualifying their entire team), and its pretty unusual to do it back-to-back. I'm really gratified; the girls really stepped up and played well."

At state, the girls once again finished third place. Whitney Hamilton finished seventh in singles, and her teammate Cat Huang finished eighth. Baxter and Brownback finished sixth place, and the other doubles team of Munker and Hirsch placed tenth at state.

Again, the depth of Washburn Rural paid dividends accumulating team points.

2004—SOPHOMORE HUANG WINS REGIONAL SINGLES TITLE

It might be a strange thought that a tennis team could win their regional but not win their city or league championship. Yet, that is just what the 2004 tennis team did.

Led by Catherine "Cat" Huang, who captured the singles championship, Washburn Rural won their regional meet. Huang beat her opponent 6-3, 6-2 to run her record to 19-5.

Laura Marshall and Cassie Edwards placed third in doubles competition.

"We had a good day," Hedberg told the Capital-Journal reporter, "We scored with our other doubles team and, after three days in Derby, we're pretty happy to be home." Hedberg describes this competition as being a part of the longest weekend of his life.

The other doubles team to win a match and score another team point was the duo of Shannon Underwood and Caitlin Corbin. The nine team points put the Junior Blues ahead of runners up Manhattan, Junction City and Wichita East—all tied with six team points.

Although there would not be a strong showing at the state tournament, sophomore Huang who won her regional singles event, finished second in the city and third at the league meet. A really good season for Huang individually.

2005—A DASH OF TEXAS WELCOMED: LONE STAR TRANSFER HELPS RURAL

When you add a transfer to an already good group of tennis players, the team gets stronger. When you add a sophomore that is good enough to take over the duties of the number one singles player, you have the makings of something really good. That was the Rural story in 2005.

In a preseason Capital-Journal article titled "Defending City Champ Trojans Reloading," their coach, Duane Pomeroy, was very grateful for the players he had at Topeka High who helped the school win five of the last seven city championships. However, Pomeroy knew his Trojans were hit hard by graduation. He said, "They (Rural) should be the favorite."

The 2005 version of Washburn Rural girls tennis captured all three big meets—city, league and regionals.

Sophomore Sheri Olivier, a Texas transfer, captured the city singles title in the Centennial League meet, but Washburn Rural really needed to go deep to complete their scoring. A seventh-place finish for their doubles team helped the Junior Blues eke out a championship by the narrowest of margins, 56-54 over Topeka West.

Cat Huang took third in the other singles competition, losing to teammate Olivier in the semifinals. Olivier beat Hayden's Alex O'Neal—a very solid player in her own right—8-3. Hayden competed in the 4A state classification based on enrollment.

An interesting side story: At this juncture in Kansas high school tennis, there really wasn't any stipulation about uniforms. In other words, the players had some control over what they wore in matches. Apparently, as a result of players' clothing and photos from this tournament, the next season, the High School Activities Association adopted a dress code for tennis wear, and bare midriff tops were disallowed.

Going into the doubles competition, Topeka West needed two victories and needed Rural to lose both matches. Rural had to sweat out some anxious moments, but the doubles duo of Shannon Underwood and Laura Marshall finished seventh with an 8-4 win.

Rural's head coach, Hedberg, spoke about the depth of his tennis team. "We have good doubles teams, two seniors who weren't with us today and the other two teams who were with us." Hedberg also went on to say, "We've been able to combine them throughout the year to get enough points to win seven out of eight meets."

The fact that the league championship was so close came as no surprise to Hedberg. "We have a lot of respect for Topeka West and knew they would be tough to beat."

In a Capital-Journal article about the regional meet, the newspaper reported that "not everything fell Washburn Rural's way, but more than enough went right to come away with the regional crown."

Rural qualified three of the four events and topped Junction City by a team score of 12-6.

"We had a really good day," Rural head coach Kevin Hedberg said. "We thought we'd win it, but we were kind of on pins and needles with our doubles for awhile."

In singles, Sheri Olivier and Cat Huang captured first and third place. Olivier defeated a Wichita Southeast player 6-0, 6-2. The doubles team of Shannon Underwood and Laura Marshall took third place in doubles to round out the scoring. All four would compete at the state tournament.

At state, Sophomore Olivier finished fourth in singles in her first appearance at the Kansas 6A championships.

2006—DEPTH THE THEME FOR RURAL'S GIRLS TENNIS

In Rick Peterson's Capital-Journal city tennis capsule for 2006, Peterson writes, "Coach Kevin Hedberg would never complain about having too many tennis players." Peterson wrote that the Junior Blues had seventeen who could possibly fit into the varsity picture this fall season.

Hedberg told Peterson, "It is a blessing and a curse. We're awfully deep and my number 11, 12 and 13-ranked players are potentially very good players, and the season's so short you just can't get enough competition (for them)." One of Hedberg's challenges was getting them all on the courts enough to be able to compete.

This year's edition of the Junior Blues saw the team returning twelve experienced players from 2005—a team that won city, league and regionals and finished fourth at the state tournament.

Their two best singles players return—junior Sherri Olivier, who finished fourth at state in '05, along with senior Catherine Huang. Hedberg made mention that he might move Huang to doubles as he tinkered with the depth of this squad. As usual, the team's goal was to improve their finish from last year's state tournament—a fourth place team finish.

"We finished a point or two out of third place last year, and fourth is the worst place to finish because you get nothing for it (team trophy wise). We'd like to move up if we can." Given the fact that Olivier and Huang returned, along with seniors Laura Marshall, Caroline Zeller and Vicki Owens who join junior returning players Cassie Edwards, Laura Caby, Rachel Butler, Jamie Hertling, Erika Munker, Elizabeth Werner and Grace Lancaster, that seemed possible.

Hedberg cautioned, "We have a solid nucleus returning, and the competition for the top six spots will be intense. I like (this team) a lot. It's a fun group and they're good girls, and we don't have to worry about anything about the classes or anything. They just take care of business, and they genuinely seem to like each other."

Inclement weather caused a meet cancellation, so Rural was the last city team to start the season, but at the Seaman Invitational, they took the top spots in three events. Number one doubles was the only event they failed to win. Olivier cruised to a 6-1 victory over her Marysville foe. Freshman Avery Clifton, who snuck in over some experienced Rural players, captured the number two singles event, defeating her Marysville opponent 6-0. In number two doubles, Edwards and Caby defeated the Junction City team 6-1. The number one doubles team of Huang and Marshall finished second to a good Junction City duo, 6-2. Incidentally, weather delays and relocation of the event prolonged the day/evening. The invitational finished at 11:30 p.m. on a Tuesday night. Marysville's team got home at 1:30 a.m.

The Junior Blues once again captured the city event, taking three of the four events. Olivier and Clifton captured the number one and number two singles events. Olivier defeated her "hitting partner" from Hayden, Alex O'Neal, 6-4, 6-1. Clifton defeated a Topeka West player 6-3, 6-1.

Hedberg was worried about the strength of that year's Topeka West tennis team. After the meet, he said, "I have a tremendous respect for West's team. They're very good and they work hard at it, and they do all the things right. I'm always a little worried. I was worried when the season started."

Even though the number one doubles team was the only second-place finisher, Hedberg was encouraged, saying, "I was very pleased with the overall effort. My number one doubles team of Marshall and Huang improved and is improving all the time like we thought they would." Dicus and Doole of Topeka West won that event 6-2, 7-5. The number two doubles team of Caby and Edwards defeated their Hayden competition 7-5, 6-4.

Washburn Rural defeated Topeka West 30-23 for the city championship.

Just a week later the Junior Blues also captured the Centennial League team title. Once again, Olivier defeated O'Neal for the number one singles title, while her teammate Clifton finished third in the number two singles competition. The Junior Blues got a fifth-place finish in doubles from Marshall and Huang, and their teammates Edwards and Caby finished sixth. Washburn Rural took the team title by ten points with 84 to Topeka West's 74.

"This was good," Hedberg reflected on this team's league finish. "The singles players have done great all year, and Avery and Sheri did their jobs today very well. In doubles, I was hoping that we could maybe break through to the top four, but I'm real pleased with how they turned out, and we're set now for what our real goal has been all year, which is the regional." They wouldn't have to wait long for that opportunity because it was just two days away.

"I like the league format," Hedberg commented, "but I wish we had it spaced a little differently. You don't know whether to practice tomorrow or give them the day off. They're going to be sore, they're going to be behind in school, and then we are getting in a van and driving to Derby on Wednesday night. I just wish there was a little bit more gap in the schedule."

Rural captured their fifth straight regional championship and looked like a top three team heading into the state tournament.

Before heading down the turnpike for Derby—the location of the state tournament—Coach Hedberg did a little figuring on paper and felt like his team had a good shot at a top three trophy finish. *If* everyone played well. Actually, he needed them to play to the best of their abilities. They did just that.

The doubles teams of Cat Huang and Laura Marshall and their teammates Cassie Edwards and Laura Caby brought home medals, which meant a strong finish by Sheri Olivier in singles could ensure Rural a top three finish.

The road that Olivier had to navigate was a treacherous one. She went three sets with a very tough Blue Valley North opponent, Taylor Fourmier. This earned her the right to play undefeated Olathe East sophomore Haley Craig who was the 2005 defending state champion in singles. According to Capital-Journal special reporter Pat Sangimino's article, the semifinal match contained some drama. Both Olivier and Craig received warnings from the line judges for outbursts. Olivier took the first set.

Olivier had this to say about the emotions of the semi-final, "We're both competitive players. We both want to win so badly." Olivier said that Haley Craig was one of those players who can get frustrated on the inside, but keep it together on the outside. But with the score tied at 4 in the decidedly lengthy set—which had eight deuces before Olivier finally took control to win the fifth—Craig threw her racket into the fence. The line judge informed her that that action would cost her a point, and a tirade on Craig's part ensued. The aftermath was her serving but losing the first three points and then hitting the final point over the fence, giving Olivier the win and a berth in the championship match.

The lengthy two matches against the caliber of players Olivier faced caused her to run out of gas in the final match, and she lost to Mary Weatherholt of Shawnee Mission South, but Olivier's second-place finish assured Washburn Rural of a second-place team finish and a state trophy.

Unfortunately for the Rural tennis program, Olivier did not play tennis for Washburn Rural in the fall of her senior year. In December her family relocated to Houston, Texas, and she went on to compete during the Texas season in the spring and played in college as well. Hedberg can only speculate, but he feels certain that she had a great shot at winning the 2007 state singles championship.

2007—GIRLS END UP WITH FOUR UNDERCLASSMEN IN TOP SIX PLAYERS

The 2007 edition of the Junior Blues didn't miss a beat. They won the three major championships. They captured the city event (albeit a team tie with Topeka West), won the Centennial League tournament, and won their seventh straight regional event.

In the city event, Hayden's Alex O'Neal captured the individual honors, winning the singles event. O'Neal added this to her already glowing resume—two-time 4A state champion, three-time state placer. Washburn Rural graduate Sheri Olivier was in O'Neal's way the last two seasons, but in her absence, O'Neal beat Washburn Rural sophomore sensation Avery Clifton. Clifton's sophomore teammate Shelby Williams also finished second in the number two singles event.

One of Rural's most consistent players in doubles, Cassie Edwards, missed the event with an injury. Caby and Hertling finished second in number one doubles. Hertling filled in for the injured Edwards. The number two Junior Blue's doubles team, which was freshman Taylor Smith and sophomore Allison Bruner, won the number two doubles event. This allowed Rural and Topeka West to both have 26 team points for a city tie for the championship. There is no tiebreaker for this event.

In a Capital-Journal article by sportswriter Rick Peterson, Peterson mentioned the, "tons of titles the Junior Blues have won over the past years." In this article he said about this season's league event, "The Junior Blues took a different route to the Centennial League girls championship Monday at Kossover Tennis Center, winning with depth."

Hayden's O'Neal once again captured the singles title, and Topeka West doubles team of Ellen Dicus and Annie Doole captured the doubles championship. But Rural carved out enough placings to defeat Topeka West 80-77 for their sixth team league title in the last seven years.

Hedberg told Peterson, "We've usually been able to get a title or two (in the events), but this year the field is so split up and, really, we're all very bunched up together. It kind of came down to depth at a couple of positions, and that made the difference."

Avery Clifton finished third in singles, and the doubles team of Laura Caby and Cassie Edwards placed third in doubles. Add a sixth-place finish in singles by freshman Alexa Hertling and also a sixth-place finish in doubles by Allison Bruner and Taylor Smith, and that gave the Junior Blues their third straight league team title.

A week before, West and Rural tied for the city championship, but with the additional teams—three schools—depth matters. Hedberg diplomatically declared, "It's just winning one or two matches here or there. We (West and Rural) could line up again tomorrow and play this thing again and lose." When you add Emporia, Junction City and Manhattan, it changes the distribution of points and rewards good depth up and down your lineup.

Depth apparently also counts in the eight-team regional event. Once again, at the regional event, Rural failed to win either singles or doubles, but defeated second-place Junction City 12-7 for the team victory.

Rural qualified its entire team for the state tournament. Hedberg said, "I'm tremendously pleased for our young kids—my two sophomores and two freshmen." Hedberg mentioned that it gives him another ten days to work with his young team and mentioned that the experience they will get playing on the big stage at the state event will help them in the future. Do you think Hedberg looks with optimism at every turn?

It was no surprise that Clifton, Edwards and Caby qualified for the state event, but getting the others in was a huge bonus. Clifton ended up playing teammate Hertling for the consolation match. Clifton defeated Hertling for third-place, and Hertling claimed fourth. Caby and Edwards made it to the championship match, finishing second, dropping a 6-3, 6-3 match to a solid Wichita East doubles team. Bruner and Smith went three sets in the third-place doubles match before dropping it 6-4, 2-6, 6-2 to the third-place Junction City duo.

Rural failed to place top three at the 6A state tournament, but the future looked very bright with four of the six players returning as they were freshmen and sophomores. One who follows Rural tennis would have to wonder what the outcome of the season would have been with Olivier on the team.

Hedberg called Danielle Knipp possibly the best tennis player in Kansas to never capture a state championship. Knipp finished 3rd her first two-years and second the next two.

(Photo credit: *Topeka Capital-Journal*)

Knipp was as good with her short game as she was with her hard volleying strokes which made her a national champion.

(Photo credit: *Topeka Capital-Journal*)

(Top) This bunch from 1993 were very close and not opposed to having fun which Coach Hedberg supported as long as they brought their "lunch pail" to practices and matches. Left to Right: Hedberg, Pendley, Van Vlack, McBride, Roberts, Lee and prone position Knipp.

(Bottom) Sherri Olivier was an aggressive left-handed player with plenty of power. She played three years at Rural before transferring her senior year proving to be the best while in Topeka.
(Photo credit: *Topeka Capital-Journal*)

In 1994 after three years of doubles play Hedberg let Megan McBride play number one singles at the Centennial League championship. She won 6-0 over her competitor.
(Photo credit: *Topeka Capital-Journal*)

Sherri Olivier, a transfer from Texas, here winning the Centennial League singles event in 2005.

(Photo credit: *Topeka Capital-Journal*)

Senior Emily Lee helped Rural win the city championship and placed ninth at the 1996 state tournament. Lee won the city singles title.

Michell Hollins, Erin Underwood and Cheryl Catron enjoy dinner after the 1997 state tournament. Catron and Hollins placed fourth in doubles, Unerwood was 13th in singles. Over a two-year period Hollins and Catron compiled a 41-10 record.

(Top) In 1999 Kristin Underwood teamed with Mindi Lewis to capture third place in doubles at the state tournament.

(Bottom) 1998 version of the lady Junior Blues tennis team finished ninth at the state tournament.

In 2003 Whitney Hamilton finished seventh place in singles at the state tournament.

2003 Abby Brownback and Kassie Baxter playing doubles in Wamego. They went on to place 6th at state.

(Photo credit: *Topeka Capital-Journal*)

(Top) 2003 Abby Brownback, Cat Huang, Kristen Munker, Aubrey Hirsch, Kassie Baxter and Whitney Hamilton hoisting the 3rd place trophy from state.

(Bottom) The 2007 doubles team of Cassie Edwards (returning) and Laura Caby were runner up at regional, but their 2nd place finish was one key to Rural capturing their 6A regional title.

(Photo credit: *Topeka Capital-Journal*)

(Top) 2008 The team carried their own captions for this picture but not their correct names. Left to right: Laura Caby, Cassie Edwards, Allison Bruner, Taylor Smith and Lexi Hertling.

(Bottom) 2010 Somewhere in the mid-nineties, the activities association loosened up the rules applying to coaching during a competition. Here's Coach giving some advice to his players.

In 2010 senior Taylor Smith had a great singles season winning city, league and regionals titles. She added a 3rd place finish at the state tournament.

Gwen Shepler and Mackenzie Hill at Kossover winning doubles at the Centennial League event in 2011.

(Photo credit: *Topeka Capital-Journal*)

2012 Mackenzie Hill makes a return volley.

In 2012 Madeline Hill won the city and league singles titles and became the first Topekan to win the prestigious singles event at the St. Thomas Aquinas' Invitational.
(Photo credit: *Topeka Capital-Journal*)

2013 Melaina Piyassaphan (pictured) and Irene Nicolas captured the number one city and league double events.

(Photo credit: *Topeka Capital-Journal*)

Senior Madeline Hill (2014) not only had to battle expectations she was dealing with tennis-elbow her senior year but capped off four wins in singles at city, league and regionals for an unprecedented career. Add a state championship and a runner-up plus two top four finishes at 6A state and you may have "a once-in a generation player"" as Hedberg called her.
(Photo credit: *Topeka Capital-Journal*)

2015 favorite Hedberg sayings.

Coaching Legacy of Champions

2019 Regional champions Left to right: Meredith Kucera, Kate Fritz, Sheridan Wichman, Grace Bradbury, Hailey Beck. Second Row: Halley Robinett and Coach Hedberg.

2020 Mena DiMarzio making a return played number two singles.

2008—EARNS EIGHTH STRAIGHT REGIONAL TITLE

In 2008 Washburn Rural had more depth than they could possibly utilize in varsity matches. You're only allowed six players. Those six players swept the city events and captured the team title by a score of 32-21, Hayden finishing second.

By capturing the city championship it marked their third in a row.

The junior singles tandem of Avery Clifton and Shelby Williams took first place in the number one and number two singles events. As a freshman, the year before, Clifton had won the number two singles event.

Clifton split her time between two sports—tennis and cross country. And her two unselfish coaches were happy to accommodate that. Hedberg told the Capital-Journal, "I'm no expert on running, but 'Shuff' (Scott Shuffelberger), head cross country coach at Washburn Rural, told me right away that he thought she had a real talent (long distance running). If you've got a kid like that, that's part of our job in high school to identify kids' talents and let those talents come through." Both of those coaches put the best interest of the kid first when other coaches might expect them to specialize. Not these two gentlemen.

Also, at city, the Junior Blues swept the doubles events. Hertling and Schwartz won the number one doubles championship defeating Topeka West's Adrienne Hearrell and Sarah Schneider. The number two doubles team of Smith and Bruner defeated Hayden's Libby Michel and Mackenzie LaCount.

"My doubles teams got some scares, which is good," Hedberg said. "They need that."

The Centennial League championship looked like it was a two team race between Rural and Topeka West. Rural's depth proved to be the difference. Hayden's Alex O'Neal proved to be the league's best singles player. Rural's Avery Clifton captured third in the consolation side. West had the league's best doubles team of Ellen Dicus and Annie Doole, but again, Rural took third in doubles with the senior team of Laura Caby and Cassie Edwards, capturing the consolation side. In the end, it was enough for Washburn Rural to outscore West 80-77 in a close team finish. The league team title was Rural's third in a row, giving them six out of the last seven years.

In Rick Peterson's Capital-Journal article, Hedberg told Peterson, "We've usually been able to get a title or two, but this year the field is so split up and really we're all very bunched up together." Hayden scored 69 team points and Seaman 67 for a very close finish. Hedberg went on to say, "It kind of came down to depth at a couple of positions, and that made the difference."

The depth that really helped push Rural to the win included freshman Lexi Hertling's sixth-place finish in the singles event coupled with the doubles pair of Taylor Smith and Allison Bruner's sixth-place finish. Washburn Rural's depth proved the difference.

"It's just winning one or two matches here or there," Hedberg said. "We could line up again tomorrow and play this thing again and lose."

Washburn Rural seemed primed and ready for regionals. This year, they played at Kossover. Rick Peterson of the Capital-Journal summed up the championship for Rural in the lead paragraph saying, "Sometimes a team can be dominant without really dominating."

Just like the previous league championship, Rural failed to win singles but still captured the team title 12-6 over Wichita Southeast. It was Rural's seventh straight regional title and Rural qualified five of its six players for the 6A state meet.

Clifton placed second in singles competition. The doubles team of Bruner and Smith captured the doubles competition, and their teammates of Hertling and Schwartz finished in third place.

"I'm tremendously pleased for our young kids, my two sophomores and two freshmen. It gives them another ten days of tennis this season, and it gives them the ability to get them on a bigger stage where they can deal with nerves and deal with all that goes along with being at a state tournament. It's just huge for us." Hedberg added, "Bruner and Smith have just gotten better all season, and they beat a very good team from Manhattan to go (to state)."

The 6A state tournament was an experience for the young Junior Blues as four underclassmen learned what state competition is all about and all five of their players finished top ten for a third place team finish.

Washburn Rural got sixth place finishes by Clifton in singles and also the doubles team of Hertling and Schwartz. Smith and Bruner started out shaky, but recovered for a ninth-place doubles finish.

According to Hedberg, the top two team finishers, champion Shawnee Mission East and Blue Valley North, "are better than we are." He went on to say, "We want to think that we want to be included in the mix and we took that step today. Things just worked out for us."

Playing on that stage, with the opportunity to return after a year of growth, maturity and experience, has to be good thing for any competitor. Competing at the state level is always good for young players. They'll know what to expect the next time they have the opportunity.

Incidentally, Avery Clifton would later win the 6A cross country championship, running the course in a time of 14.59.91, beating the next best runner from Manhattan by almost ten seconds.

2009–RURAL CLAIMS FIFTH CONSECUTIVE CITY TITLE

Rural lost four of its top six players from 2008. Three to graduation and one, Avery Clifton, to another sport. Clifton was a premier distance runner in both cross country and track, and managed to balance competing in BOTH tennis AND cross country the last two fall seasons. More on that later.

With so many newcomers, Rural had a great tuneup for the city championship with their own invitational, winning 50-39 over Hayden in the nine-team event.

While not winning the city title alone, the Junior Blues played well enough to share the title with both Topeka West and Hayden. Senior Allison Bruner and junior Taylor Smith were the city number one doubles champions. Their teammates, sophomore Gwen Shepler and freshman Mackenzie Hill, finished second in number two doubles. Junior Christy Peterson earned a third-place finish in number two singles.

Rural's Hedberg was just fine with sharing the city title. "I'm very happy for our girls. I thought we could be anywhere from first to second to third, but I was really leaning more toward second or third. It was incredibly close," Hedberg told Capital-Journal sportswriter Rick Peterson.

With some confidence Topeka West gained from the city championship, West ended Rural's string of Centennial League championships. West's team score of

83 came despite not winning any of the four individual events. Washburn Rural finished with 77, and Bruner and Smith won the city doubles championship. All of West's players finished in the top six to rack up the 83 points. Depth.

Topeka Capital-Journal sportswriter Brent Maycock mentioned in his lead paragraph, "Not everything went exactly as Washburn Rural tennis coach Kevin Hedberg had hoped (at regionals). But enough went right for the Junior Blues to win their ninth consecutive regionals crown." Washburn Rural swept the top two places in singles and qualified their entire team for the state meet. Rural took the regional team title, distancing Manhattan's team score 23-13. Maria Stoica topped her teammate Christy Peterson for first and second in singles. Bruner and Smith finished second in doubles. Shepler and Mackenzie Hill finished fourth in doubles. Hedberg told Maycock, "We're a young team. We could have done a little better but we got everyone through and things went pretty well for us."

Smith and Bruner finished sixth at 6A state in doubles.

The rest of the story . . .

Avery Clifton was a talented multi-sport athlete who had pulled double duty with two sports her junior year during her high school career. A standout in tennis, Clifton's best sport was cross country and the distance races in track. So when Clifton made her decision to bypass her senior year of tennis, Coach Hedberg had to know that he had some big shoes to fill with a replacement. Next gal up.

Here is Clifton's (a 2010 graduate) account of the difficult part of that decision. "I first met Coach Hedberg when I was in third or fourth grade, so around 2000 or 2001. I participated in his summer tennis camps at Washburn Rural High School (WRHS) and these camps were formative in my early tennis days. I remember looking forward to the day that I could hopefully play under Heberg in high school. I ended up playing for him my freshman through my junior years at WRHS. We went to state as a team all three years, and I have many fond memories of these seasons. The fall of my junior year, I both played tennis and ran cross country for the first time. Hedberg was very gracious to me in letting me do this, and he was always very encouraging to me in my up-and-coming running career. For my senior year, I had to make a tough decision, and ultimately ended up choosing not to play tennis so that I could focus on cross country. I remember the day I told Hedberg. I think I cried when I told him because I felt so bad about letting him down, but he didn't make me feel bad at all. Rather he was encouraging and told me he wanted me to pursue running as he knew I loved it and had talent. I felt so grateful in this moment. This is exactly the person Hedberg is. Selfless, humble, kind. Thank you Hedberg for being such a wonderful example to me and thousands of other kids over the years of not only how to be a good tennis player, but how to be a good person. You will be missed (at Rural)."

2010—A NEW CENTENNIAL LEAGUE STREAK WOULD REACH EIGHT STRAIGHT

Coming off a sixth-place finish at state in 2009, Rural returned a good nucleus and added some solid newcomers for their first season of the decade. In a preseason look at the upcoming season put together by the Capital-Journal, Hedberg said, "We have a deep team with good potential. We expect our league to be competitive and difficult. As usual, we will need good senior leadership."

With that mention of senior leadership, senior Taylor Smith—who had been involved in three previous city team championships—added a first number one singles title to make it four team city championships, and Rural ran their streak of city championships to ten. Smith had played her Hayden opponent just a week earlier. Smith said, "It helped to know her style of game I guess and just know how she plays. But she knows how I play too, so she had that advantage too."

Maria Stoica took second place at the city event, and it was a sweep of the doubles events with Mackenzie Hill and Gwen Shepler capturing the number one doubles event, while teammates and seniors Gabriella Hirsch and Christy Peterson won the number two doubles event. Rural outdistanced second-place Hayden by a score of 30-21.

10

TEACHING, TAMING, AND TRANSIT TROUBLES

My second year of teaching was, without a doubt, the wildest ride of my professional life. I found myself assigned to a specialist reception centre – a halfway house of sorts for boys aged ten to fourteen, each carrying a tangled mix of social, emotional, and behavioural challenges. Offenders and non-offenders were thrown together in this melting pot, and the only guarantee was unpredictability.

Some of these boys were wards of the state, waiting for adoption or foster homes; others were bouncing between orphanages and mental health facilities, sometimes even awaiting trial. Their stays ranged from mere days to a handful of months, which meant that just as you started to remember someone's name, they'd be gone – or replaced by someone with an even more creative way of causing chaos.

The most common battles we faced were with oppositional defiant disorder (ODD), conduct disorder (CD), and attention deficit hyperactivity disorder (ADHD).

Traditional teaching methods? Out the window. Instead, I became part educator, part life coach, and full-time wrangler. I overhauled the curriculum to focus on life skills – conflict resolution, teamwork, and even how not to use your shoelaces for mischief. To help manage behaviours, I introduced a points system: good choices earned rewards, and, if all went to plan, a weekly field trip. Their crowning achievement? Earning a visit to the local zoo.

The big day arrived, and our chariot awaited: a battered old Ford Transit van with a key that looked like it had fought a losing battle with a garbage disposal. Still, with the zoo just a few kilometres away, I decided to gamble.

Outings with this crew were always a high-stakes adventure. There was every chance that someone would vanish over a fence or attempt to ride a meerkat. But to my utter amazement, they were model citizens – at least for the day. We had a blast at the zoo, marvelling at animals and only mildly alarming the staff.

But as we gathered to leave, disaster struck: the van wouldn't start. I jiggled the key, coaxed, pleaded – nothing. Panic crept in. If we didn't make it back on time, the next ride might be in a police car. And, of course, this was before the age of cellphones, so calling for help was out of the question.

Sensing my distress – and perhaps eager to avoid a night at the zoo – my students sprang into action. 'Don't worry, Robert. We'll fix it!' they declared with the confidence only boys who've watched too many heist movies can muster. Within minutes, a couple of them were under the dashboard, wires crossed, and – voilà! – the engine roared to life. I wasn't sure whether to be impressed or concerned, but I learned something important that day: never underestimate a group of resourceful kids with a questionable moral compass.

Since then, I've lived by one rule: always expect the unexpected. And maybe, just maybe, learn a thing or two about hotwiring.

11

A STICKY SITUATION: THE CASE OF THE VANISHING ADHESIVE

Keeping the boys at the specialist reception centre motivated and engaged in their work was never a straightforward task. No matter what I tried, their attention wandered faster than socks disappeared in a washing machine.

So, in a flash of inspiration (or perhaps desperation), I decided to shake things up and introduced model-building activities.

Suddenly, my classroom was transformed into a hive of creativity, with boys assembling, painting, and gluing together intricate models of planes, ships, and tanks. The tables were littered with tiny wheels, wings, and enough paint to redecorate the staffroom twice over.

It didn't take long for the buzz to spread. Soon, other groups were clamouring to join in, eager to get their hands on some glue and a plastic Spitfire. I was quietly congratulating myself for having discovered the Holy Grail of classroom engagement.

But then a mystery emerged. Despite my frequent glue runs – I was on first-name terms with the cashier at the craft shop – there was never enough glue to go around. It was as if the glue had sprouted legs and made a dash for freedom every night.

Eventually, the truth came out, and it was stickier than I'd imagined. Some of the boys had developed a penchant for glue sniffing and were stealthily 'liberating' tubes of glue for their own recreational use. My brilliant plan had gone up in fumes.

Back to the drawing board, I switched out the gluey models for Lego bricks, hoping for another spark of enthusiasm. But as any seasoned teacher will tell you, you can lead a horse to Lego, but you can't make it care. The boys' interest fizzed out faster than my supply of glue had. Ah well, not every experiment is a roaring success – sometimes, all you can do is pick up the pieces (or the Lego bricks) and try again.

12

SECRETS BEHIND THE DOG FLAP

During my stint at the specialist reception centre, I quickly realised it was less of a holding facility and more of an unintentional comedy club, its stage packed with pint-sized, would-be outlaws. The boys there didn't just recount their escapades – they competed to outdo each other, each story more outrageous than the last, delivered with the brazen honesty of those who'd already run out of things to lose and could only gain in laughter.

One rainy afternoon stands out the most. The day dragged on, rain tapping the windows like it was bored too, when a wiry boy with a grin stretching dangerously wide sidled up to me. There was a gleam in his eye – the kind that signals a brilliant story, an impending disaster, or both. Without any prompting, he launched into a detailed retelling of a burglary attempt he and a mate had pulled in one of those posh neighbourhoods where the lawns are manicured and the dogs have Instagram followers.

They had spent days casing the place, he explained, hiding in hedges and playing lost paperboys whenever someone got suspicious. 'We were like ninjas, Robert!' he declared, puffing his chest. 'Except, you know, clumsier and starving.' When the owners finally left for work, they made their move. Forget lock-picking or smashing windows – these budding criminal geniuses chose the dog flap. I nearly spat out my tea as he described their attempts to squeeze through, limbs flailing, looking more like a pair of oversized, criminally-inclined Jack Russells than anything else. 'You'd be amazed what desperation can do,' he said with a conspiratorial wink.

Once inside, they tore the house apart: drawers yanked open, cupboards emptied, bed sheets tossed around like confetti at a particularly chaotic wedding. After an hour of frantic searching, their haul amounted to old receipts, expired gift cards, and a mysterious pair of socks. Hungry and thoroughly unimpressed, they turned their attention to the kitchen. There, they raided the fridge with the subtlety of raccoons, managing to scrape together a sorry feast: a few limp slices of deli meat, wilted lettuce, and a battered tub of margarine. 'We made sandwiches – if you could call them that,' he said. 'Honestly, I think the bread was older than I am.'

The story took a cinematic turn just as he was about to slather margarine on a slice. Popping open the tub, he found not butter, but a stash of watches and jewellery sparkling like pirate treasure. 'We thought we'd hit the jackpot! he crowed, eyes alight. 'Turns out, sometimes the real treasure really is hidden in the world's dodgiest butter tub.'

Of course, their stroke of luck eventually ran out. The police were not convinced by their stories of dairy products and spontaneous picnics. Following a brief but spirited pursuit, the boys were apprehended. The stolen goods remained hidden – possibly in yet another unsuspecting kitchen container.

Unable to help myself, I leaned in and asked, 'So, where did you stash the loot?' dropping my voice like we were partners in crime. He just flashed that irrepressible grin and replied, 'I'm not telling. I've done the crime, and when I've done the time, whatever's left is mine.'

With that, he swaggered off, leaving me to wonder whether I had just met a future criminal mastermind – or the next stand-up comedian.

13

BINOCULARS, BUSINESS, AND BRIAN: THE SEAL DEAL

School camps are where childhood memories are made. There's something magical about being whisked away from the everyday routine and plunged into a world of adventure – nature hikes, thrilling activities, and lungs full of crisp, fresh air. I've attended my fair share of unforgettable camps, but none left a mark quite like the Phillip Island trip. And that was all thanks to a fifth-grader named Brian – a boy with a sharp mind, boundless confidence, and more entrepreneurial spirit than most adults.

From the moment we arrived, Brian was just as captivated as the rest of us. The sweeping coastal views took our breath away, and our visit to the koala sanctuary was a highlight. That day, Brian carried his grandfather's fancy binoculars everywhere, but curiously, he never once raised them to his eyes. I couldn't figure out why he was lugging them around like a prized trophy.

All became clear when our bus finally rolled up to the southwest tip of Phillip Island – Seal Rocks. Eagerly, we filed off the bus and made our way along the boardwalk, buzzing with excitement to see Australia's biggest fur seal colony basking in the sun.

This, it turned out, was Brian's moment of glory. With a dramatic flourish, he whipped out the binoculars and trained them on the seals, gasping and exclaiming as if he'd discovered a hidden treasure. Instantly, a crowd of classmates formed, all clamouring for a turn. Brian, ever the businessman, saw his opportunity. 'Twenty cents a go!' he announced, waving the binoculars enticingly. Before we knew it, a queue had formed – and Brian was happily collecting coins, one seal-watching turn at a time.

By the end of the day, Brian had made a small fortune and cemented his place in camp legend. As for the rest of us, we learned that at school camp, the real adventure sometimes comes from the unexpected – and from classmates who know how to spot an opportunity, even among the seals.

14

FRACTIONS: HASTA LA VISTA, WHOLE NUMBERS

Teaching fractions has always been a daunting and time-consuming task, but every teacher knows how essential it is for students to master this skill as they move on to more advanced maths. Working with fractions sharpens students' mathematical minds, helping them tackle arithmetic problems with growing confidence and accuracy.

Still, I was surprised to see just how far understanding fractions could stretch a young mind.

It was my third-graders' first introduction to fractions, and excitement (with a dash of confusion) buzzed in the air. I started with the basics: 'We use fractions instead of whole numbers when we want to talk about just a part of something,' I explained, gesturing to the diagram on the board.

All eyes were on me as I broke it down further. 'There are three parts to a fraction,' I said. 'First, the numerator – the number above the bar. Second, the denominator – the number below the bar. And the third part is –'

Before I could finish, one student jumped in with impeccable comedic timing: 'The Terminator, played by Arnold Schwarzenegger!'

The room erupted in laughter. My own composure slipped, and I had to make a hasty exit to the hallway, grinning from ear to ear.

'Where are you going, Mr Fav?' another student called after me, barely stifling giggles.

Without missing a beat, I channelled my inner action hero and replied, in my best Arnold Schwarzenegger voice, 'Don't worry, I'll be back!'

15

BILLY'S GUIDE TO NOT GETTING MELTED

'What do you want to be when you grow up? A performer? A doctor? Maybe even a secret agent?' I asked, scanning the sea of eager faces in my first-grade classroom. Their eyes sparkled with the kind of wild ambition only six-year-olds can muster, each one brimming with dreams shaped by cartoons, superheroes, and the stories their parents told at bedtime.

Hands shot up like rockets. 'A ballerina!' 'A fire-fighter!' 'A dinosaur!' The usual parade of charming and occasionally impossible aspirations filled the air, and I couldn't help but smile.

But Billy, with his untidy hair and sneakers that blinked with every kick under his desk, cleared his throat and announced, 'I want to be an astronaut because I want to be the first person to set foot on the sun.' He said it with such conviction that for a split second, I almost believed he could pull it off.

The classroom fell silent. The only sound was the faint hum of the air conditioner and the shuffling of crayons. Billy's best friend, Lucy, twisted in her seat, her brow furrowing with concern. 'Billy,' she said, choosing her words carefully, 'you can't land on the sun. It's way too hot. Like, it would melt you! That's never going to happen.'

Billy, undeterred, crossed his arms and leaned back, sporting a grin that said he had already solved the world's biggest problem. 'Yeah, I know it's hot,' he replied, his voice steady and confident. 'That's why I'm going to land at night!'

The room erupted with laughter. Even Lucy couldn't help but giggle at Billy's ingenious solution. After all, in the logic of first-graders, anything is possible – especially with a little imagination and a really good plan.

16

SAY CHEESE... AND HOPE FOR THE BEST

The start of a new year ushers in a beloved – and, for some, dreaded – tradition: school photo day. This annual event is a masterclass in unpredictability, immortalised in glossy prints that almost never match the polished visions parents dream of. Instead, those treasured photos are typically snapped right after recess, when hair defies gravity, shirts are rumpled, and faces are decorated with mysterious smudges – usually remnants of a chocolate chip cookie or whatever sticky snack was available.

School photographers possess a unique talent for freezing the most unexpected moments in time. Somehow, they always manage to catch mid-blink squints, lopsided grins, and wild-eyed expressions that would be right at home in a haunted house mirror. Year after year, parents open those photo envelopes with a cocktail of hope and resignation, silently wondering if this will finally be the year they get a frame-worthy shot.

This year was no different. As our class shuffled into line – bows askew, shirts untucked – Amelia, ever the practical thinker, raised her hand. 'Can you take a few extra pictures, please?' she asked the photographer, her voice tinged with hope.

The photographer, a seasoned veteran of the school photo battlefield, grinned knowingly. 'I always do,' he replied, camera at the ready.

Amelia sagged with visible relief. 'YES! Awesome!' she exclaimed, loud enough for everyone to hear as she confided, 'Because if I make a weird face, my mum makes me pay for the photos out of my pocket money.'

Watching from across the room, I couldn't help but laugh. Every year, I promise myself, 'This time will be different.' Yet, school photos somehow always capture the delightful chaos and personality of our class better than any carefully posed portrait ever could. Maybe, just maybe, that's the real tradition.

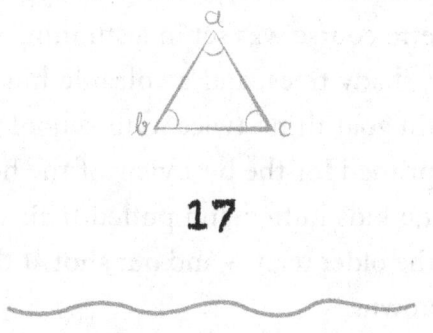

17

THE DAY TOM RAN HIS OWN RACE

My job as a physical education teacher landed me at a tiny school where our sports teams, through sheer grit and relentless training, regularly trounced their competition. We racked up championship trophies and always snagged top spots in swimming and athletics. But there was one event that forever eluded us: cross-country. The closest we ever got to victory was a hopeful sigh.

Then along came Tom – a new student, from hot and steamy far north Queensland. Tom was a runner, and not just any runner. He was a barefoot runner, with legs like springs, a smile that could light up a stadium, and a laid-back attitude that made everyone around him feel comfortable. Every lunch break, he'd rally his teammates for running drills, turning practice into equal parts laughter and sweat.

Race day dawned hot enough to fry an egg on the pavement. The two-kilometre course was set in a stunning park dotted with sparkling dams, shady trees, and a volcanic hill steep enough to make a mountain goat think twice. Our school camped out near the finish line, primed for the best view of the home straight.

After the little kids huffed and puffed their way to the finish, it was time for the older team – and our shot at that long-awaited cross-country crown.

The starter's pistol cracked through the air, and Tom shot to the front like a kangaroo on a trampoline. We hollered ourselves hoarse as he kept a blistering pace, leaving his rivals trailing in his dust. Victory was so close we could taste it – until Tom stopped dead on the dam bridge, just metres from the finish.

Before we could process what was happening, Tom launched himself off the bridge and into the water with a wild whoop. He splashed, he laughed, and he waved cheerfully at the runners streaming past, looking as if he'd found paradise.

Eventually, Tom strolled over the finish line, soaking wet and grinning from ear to ear, his T-shirt clinging to him like seaweed. Still blinking in disbelief, I asked what on earth made him stop.

With a mischievous twinkle, Tom replied, 'On a hot day, I'd rather swim than run!'

That day, we learned something better than winning. Sometimes, the coolest moments in life really do involve taking a leap – and enjoying a swim when everyone else is running.

18

SOPHIE'S DIVINE DOODLES

Drawing is more than just a way for children to pass the time with crayons and paper – it's a gateway into their wild imaginations. Not only does it spark creativity and help develop hand–eye coordination, but it also gives kids a chance to express feelings that sometimes words just can't capture.

If you really want to know what's going on inside a child's mind, take a closer look at their art. Their masterpieces can be windows into their biggest fears, happiest moments, wildest dreams, and even the monsters hiding under the bed. Sometimes, their doodles even offer a glimpse into their personalities – are they bold, imaginative, shy, or maybe just obsessed with dinosaurs?

One morning, as my prep students were busily sketching away, I wandered around the classroom, admiring the colourful chaos. The subjects were as varied as ever: families, beloved pets, magical unicorns, robots ready to save the world, and, of course, the occasional terrifying *T. Rex*.

Curious, I stopped beside Sophie, who was focusing intently on her paper. 'What are you drawing?' I asked.

Without looking up, she answered, 'I'm drawing God.'

I chuckled and said, 'But no one knows what God looks like.'

Sophie didn't even pause to think. Crayon still moving, she replied, 'They will in a minute!'

Clearly, when it comes to creativity – and confidence – kids have us all beat.

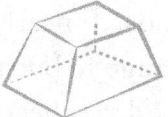

19

SPINACH, SAILORS, AND SLIP-UPS: OLIVIA'S MOVIE MIX-UP

To break the ice at the start of each school year, I like to spark conversation by asking my students about their holidays. It's usually a surefire way to hear tales of exotic trips, backyard adventures, or family traditions – stories that range from amusing to downright astonishing.

But nothing quite prepared me for Olivia's family movie night. Olivia, a vibrant five-year-old with boundless energy and an infectious smile, bounced in her seat as she recalled her favourite holiday memory.

'My parents took me to see my favourite movie!' she announced, practically glowing with excitement.

Curious, another child piped up, 'What did you see?'

Without missing a beat, Olivia declared, 'Popeye… the adult virgin!'

A moment of stunned silence hung in the air. A few kids giggled behind their hands. I nearly slid off my chair, torn between disbelief and the urge to burst out laughing.

Sensing our confusion, Olivia cheerfully continued to describe the film: a tale about the iconic sailor man, his quirky friends, and their adventures in the seaside town of Sweethaven. As she enthusiastically recounted scenes, it became clear she meant the live-action 'Popeye' movie and, in her excitement, had simply mixed up 'version' and 'virgin'.

The relief in the room was palpable. And while I've heard plenty of unforgettable holiday stories, Olivia's 'adult virgin' Popeye will always take the spinach-flavoured cake.

20

THE FAST-FORWARD APPROACH TO NAPLAN PREP

Each year, nearly a million Australian students sharpen their pencils for the NAPLAN (National Assessment Program Literacy and Numeracy) exam. This nationwide test is the yardstick for measuring students' literacy and numeracy skills, and by extension, the effectiveness of our teaching strategies. With so much riding on the results, schools feel the heat – and teachers devote countless hours to ensuring their students are ready for the big day.

One afternoon, deep in the trenches of third-grade maths revision, I stood at the chalkboard and sketched two familiar symbols: > and <. With a flourish, I turned to my eager class and asked, 'Can anyone tell me what these mean?'

Without missing a beat, one confident student shot his hand into the air. 'One is for fast-forward, and the other is for rewind!' he declared, channelling the energy of a seasoned remote-control operator.

Unable to contain my amusement, I grinned and nodded at his ingenious interpretation. 'Excellent work! From now on, you're officially in charge of all our audio and video equipment!'

Who knew that preparing for NAPLAN could be such a blast from the past – literally?

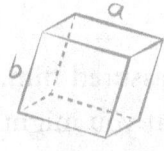

21

LUCAS AND THE LITERAL SEARCH FOR ANSWERS

To truly nurture a student's growth, teachers must keep a careful eye on progress, adjusting lessons to meet each child's developmental needs and tossing in just enough challenge to keep things interesting.

Take, for example, the time I administered a reading test to my Year 3 class. The goal? Gauge their reading and comprehension skills. The process was straightforward: read a passage, then answer a series of long, detailed questions. Simple, right? Well, not always.

Enter Lucas, the newest face in the classroom and a boy with a knack for asking the questions everyone else is thinking. As soon as I handed out the test, he stared at it, eyebrows knitted in suspicion.

'Why do I have to do this?' he asked, as though I'd just handed him a tax return.

'Just do your best,' I reassured him. 'This test will show what you already know, and what you might need to work on.'

Lucas eyed the paper as if it might bite him. 'But it's too hard!' he declared, halfway between outrage and despair.

I suggested starting with the easier questions, skipping the tough ones for now, and returning to them later. Lucas gave a dramatic sigh, the kind only eight-year-olds can truly master, and set to work. For about two minutes.

Suddenly, he slammed his pencil down. 'I still don't know the answer to this question!' he burst out.

Trying to keep things calm (and failing only a little), I said, 'Try looking for clues in the passage. Read it quietly and see if anything jumps out.'

He glared at his paper, muttered, 'You should have said that earlier,' and then – without warning – marched out of the classroom, test and pencil in hand.

After a minute, I found Lucas pacing the hallway, scanning the floor and walls with intense concentration.

'Lucas, what exactly are you doing out here?' I asked, trying to keep a straight face.

He looked up exasperated. 'You told me to search the passage for clues to find the answer! So here I am, searching the passage!'

Sometimes, it seems, instructions really do need to be crystal clear – especially when the search for clues turns into a full-on detective mission down the school corridor.

22

WHY OH Y? ALPHABET ANTICS IN ROOM PF

The alphabet is the bedrock upon which reading, writing, and spelling are built. Before children can become confident readers, they must first master every letter and its unique sound – like unlocking the secret code to the world of words.

One bright morning, sunlight streaming through the windows, we gathered in a cosy circle on the classroom carpet. Our voices blended together as we sang the ABC song for what felt like the hundredth time – some on key, some enthusiastically off. Suddenly, Flynn, who had a talent for asking questions at just the right (or wrong) moment, shot his hand into the air and asked, 'How many letters are in the alphabet?'

Before I could answer, Mia, never one to shy away from a challenge, blurted out with absolute certainty, 'It's 25!'

I couldn't help but raise an eyebrow, fighting back a smile. 'Are you sure about that?' I asked, reaching for a set of alphabet cards. 'Why don't we count them together? The English alphabet actually has 26 letters.'

Mia's face scrunched up in confusion. She shrugged, looking from the cards to me. 'Oh. I thought there were only 25. I don't know why.'

Just then, Flynn's face lit up with a mischievous grin. He leaned in and declared, 'That's because you said you don't know Y!'

The whole class erupted in giggles, and even Mia had to laugh at Flynn's clever punch line. Sometimes, it seems, learning the alphabet is just as much about the letters as it is about finding the right moment for a good joke.

23

SURVIVING NAPLAN: THE GREAT AUSSIE TEST-A-THON

Every year, like clockwork, NAPLAN sweeps through classrooms across Australia, targeting students in Years 3, 5, 7, and 9. On paper, it's a grand tool for governments, education authorities, and schools to check if young Australians are meeting those all-important educational milestones. It claims to measure the skills every child needs to survive not just school, but life itself – reading, writing, spelling, grammar, and, of course, that ever-slippery beast called numeracy.

But here's the real story: ask any teacher and you'll hear a chorus of groans. Many of us think NAPLAN is about as effective as using a ruler to measure a thunderstorm. Meanwhile, students aren't exactly celebrating either. In fact, research shows a third of them become more anxious than a cat at bath time whenever NAPLAN rolls around. For many kids, these tests are the scariest part of the whole school experience.

One of my students summed up the whole NAPLAN circus perfectly when he asked, with big, worried eyes, 'Is this the test to test us for the test to see if we are ready for the test?'

If you ask me, that's the most accurate description I've heard yet – because with all the practice tests and drills, it sometimes feels like we're in an endless loop of being tested just to get ready for being tested!

24

SHOW AND TELL OR SHOW AND YELL?

Show and tell is always a highlight in my classroom – a chance for students to bring a little piece of their world to share with their friends. Whether it's a favourite toy, a precious keepsake, or a wild tale, these moments help boost their confidence and sharpen their communication skills.

But nothing gets the students more excited than our pet-themed show and tell. The mere mention of it sends a wave of anticipation through the room. Kids can't wait to parade their furry (or scaly, or feathery) companions, sharing how they named them, how they care for them, and, of course, the hilarious or heroic stories that come with pet ownership.

Over the years, my classroom has transformed into a miniature zoo – dogs with wagging tails, purring cats, cuddly rabbits, chubby guinea pigs, glimmering fish, slow-moving tortoises, and even some mysterious axolotls. I've welcomed reptiles and insects, too, though I'll admit the insects never get quite as many hugs.

But nothing could have prepared me for Andrew's entry.

On this big show and tell day, Andrew marched in with a bug catcher in one hand and a suspicious-looking glass jar in the other. The jar's lid was secured with what looked like half a roll of tape, and inside, nestled on a twig, was a tangled web and a bustling cluster of red-backed spiders. The classroom gasped in unison – a sound somewhere between awe and outright terror.

'Would you like me to pass the jar around?' Andrew offered, with the confidence of someone who's never seen his teacher faint.

I politely declined, clutching my dignity as tightly as Andrew's mum must have clutched that tape. The kids leaned in for a better look, half curious, half ready to sprint for the exit.

Trying to keep everyone calm, I asked, 'Did you catch them with the bug catcher?'

Andrew shook his head, holding the bug catcher aloft like a vital piece of safety equipment. 'Oh, no! This is the emergency containment unit. Mum says if the jar breaks, you use this to scoop them up really fast. You know, so they don't get stepped on.' He added, helpfully, 'Or run up someone's trousers.'

Suddenly, show and tell seemed less like a classroom tradition and more like a survival challenge. Next time, I think I'll stick to goldfish.

25

A TEN OUT OF TEN FOR EFFORT

James, age five, could barely contain his excitement as he bounced to the front of the class, ready to reveal his big news. With a grin stretched from ear to ear, he announced, 'I can count to ten!' He'd spent the whole evening with his parents, practising until even the family cat looked impressed.

Standing tall, James took a dramatic breath and began, 'One, two, three…' His classmates leaned forward, eyes wide, as if he were performing a magic trick. When he reached 'ten', the room erupted in spontaneous applause. James's face lit up so brightly he might have powered the classroom lights with his smile.

'Can you count backwards?' piped up a curious classmate.

'Absolutely!' James replied, and, mishearing just a little, he counted from one to ten again – but this time he shuffled backwards across the carpet, looking very pleased with his creative interpretation.

Watching from my desk, I couldn't help but smile at James's enthusiasm. It reminded me that sometimes the joy of learning matters far more than getting everything exactly right.

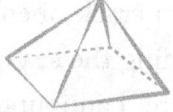

26

SPOTTING TROUBLE IN PREP ORIENTATION

Prep orientation is a whirlwind of excitement for pre-schoolers, a chance to dip their toes into the ocean of elementary school life. With a buffet of school-readiness activities on offer, these little ones eagerly collect new skills, form fast friendships, adjust to unfamiliar routines, and begin to recognise the faces of their soon-to-be teachers.

On this particular day, thanks to my colleague's unfortunate cold, I found myself at the helm of a double-sized group. The classroom transformed into Grand Central Station at rush hour, with a stampede of pint-sized students tumbling in, each determined to secure the best spot on the carpet. Some clustered around me like ducklings to their mother, while others flopped down next to their friends, chattering away.

Just as we were about to begin – packed so snugly I was half-expecting someone to crack open a can and add olive oil – I spotted a little girl scanning the sea of children.

'There's a spot right there!' I announced, feeling a bit like an air-traffic controller directing a very small but determined airplane.

With everyone settled, I launched into my welcome speech and began reading a story. Out of the corner of my eye, I noticed the same girl glancing at the floor, then up at me, her brow furrowed in confusion.

'Are you all right?' I asked gently.

She shook her head, lips pursed in an unmistakable frown.

'What seems to be the problem?' I probed, concern growing.

She sighed, exasperated. 'I can't find the spot!'

Ah, the joys of teaching – where even the simplest instructions can become complex riddles, and sometimes the only spot anyone can find is the one you never knew was missing.

27

WALLY'S VANISHING ACT (AND MY SOAKED HEROICS)

The day of the district swimming championships dawned bright and buzzing with excitement. My post for the day was lifeguard duty at the diving pool – a position I took seriously, armed with my whistle, a watchful gaze, and an acute sense of responsibility. Every diver's safety rested on my shoulders, and I was determined not to let anything slip past me.

The events rolled on, until suddenly, during the sixth-grade heats, I noticed Wally – an energetic boy known for his mischief – vanish beneath the surface. Seconds ticked by, each one feeling longer than the last. The chatter and laughter around the pool faded into a dull roar in my ears. My heart thudded as I scanned the water, searching for any sign of him. When he failed to reappear, I didn't hesitate. Fully clothed, I launched myself into the pool, arms slicing through the water as I frantically combed the depths, eyes wide, lungs burning, mind racing through every worst-case scenario.

After what felt an eternity, I surfaced, gasping for air, only to spot Wally – dripping but grinning – standing with his friends by the diving board, very much alive and well. Relief washed over me, quickly followed by a hot flush of embarrassment as I realised I was now the only one in the pool, sopping wet and fully dressed, while the crowd looked on in bewildered amusement.

'Are you all right?' I called out, trying to regain some composure.

'Yes!' Wally replied cheerfully. 'We were having a contest to see who could stay underwater the longest.' Apparently, he'd popped up just as I'd heroically dived in.

As I climbed out, clothes clinging to me like a second skin, the laughter around me grew. But my shame was short-lived – someone declared that, thanks to my impromptu performance, I'd actually won the contest for holding my breath the longest. Not quite the victory I had in mind, but I suppose every hero gets their moment – drenched or not.

28

WHEN GEOMETRY GETS HEAVENLY

Before delving into the world of angles with my fourth-grade students, I decided that a brief, low-stakes assessment was necessary. This wasn't for grading; it was a quick pre-test designed to gauge their existing understanding of basic geometric concepts, specifically angles. I wanted to see what geometric understanding lay beneath the surface of my students' minds. It's always a fascinating, and sometimes surprising, look at their current knowledge.

The question I posed was straightforward, intended to be easy and clearly worded to assess their grasp of the concept: 'Draw a picture of a triangle and show the angles.' Simple enough, I thought. I pictured neat little triangles, perhaps some less precise drawings from the less confident, but certainly the standard mathematical symbols used to denote angles marked in the corners. I eagerly gathered the papers, anticipating the usual mix.

Then came 'that' paper. The triangle was there, perfectly respectable, with sides meeting just fine. But in the corners... oh, the corners. Instead of the sharp, precise markings of angles, there were three distinct, tiny figures. Complete with halos and delicate wings. My student, bless their literal interpretation, hadn't drawn angle markings; they'd drawn miniature celestial beings.

It stopped me in my tracks. A slow smile spread across my face. It was a perfect illustration of how words can take flight in a young mind, leading to wonderfully unexpected, even angelic, interpretations. Sometimes, the most memorable responses aren't the ones you anticipate, but the ones that bring a smile and remind you just how wonderfully unpredictable teaching can be.

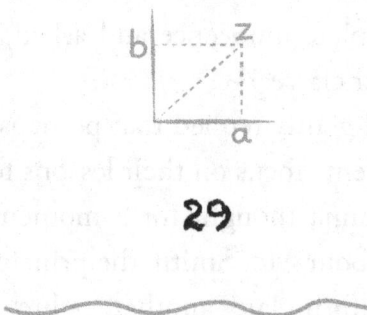

29

BREANNA AND THE UNFORGETTABLE ZUCCHINI

Breanna, a bright-eyed preparatory student, took immense pride in her flourishing vegetable garden at home. Each week, she arrived at school bearing an assortment of freshly picked produce for show and tell, her excitement as vibrant as the vegetables she carried.

One memorable morning, Breanna approached me with a grin, cradling an enormous zucchini she had just harvested. The vegetable's comically exaggerated, unmistakably suggestive shape drew immediate, barely contained laughter from the parents assisting in the classroom. Their attempts at composure only made the moment more hilarious, as giggles rippled around the room.

Once the laughter had finally died down, Breanna looked up at me with complete innocence and asked, 'Can I show my zucchini to the other classes?'

Stifling a smile, I gently replied that perhaps it would be best to let the other students focus on their lessons for now.

Undeterred, Breanna thought for a moment before brightly suggesting, 'What about Mrs Smith, the principal?'

Before I could formulate another polite refusal, Breanna was already halfway across the room, clutching the enormous vegetable like a trophy. She marched with purpose directly to the principal's office. A few moments later, the office door opened, and Mrs Smith herself emerged, not looking flustered or amused, but rather... pleased.

'Ah, Breanna!' she boomed, taking the zucchini with a professional air. 'Just the size I needed! We're having a staff bake-off today, and I'm making my famous zucchini bread. This beauty will practically guarantee me first prize!' She winked conspiratorially at me over Breanna's head, a twinkle in her eye, then turned back to the beaming student. 'Thank you so much, darling! You're a lifesaver!' And with that, she retreated back into her office, the comically suggestive zucchini tucked under her arm like a prize-winning marlin, leaving me and the now-speechless parents in the classroom staring at the closed door.

Sometimes, as a teacher, all you can do is stare, blink, and wonder if you just witnessed a giant, phallic-shaped vegetable disappear into the principal's office for a bake-off. You never really know what's going to happen next.

30

THE ABCs OF HAPPILY EVER AFTER

Five-year-old Tina, with sparkling eyes and a head full of questions, was bubbling over with excitement after watching Cinderella for the first time. She recounted every magical moment, ending with a dreamy sigh, 'Cinderella married the prince and they lived happily ever after!'

But then Tina looked up at me with a mischievous grin and asked, 'If I kiss a boy, does that mean I'm married?'

Trying not to laugh, I gently explained that marriage was a bit more complicated than a kiss – that people needed to be older and had to promise to be together forever by making special vows.

Tina furrowed her brow, clearly unconvinced. 'Why do I have to be older for vows?' she protested. 'I already know my vows: A, E, I, O, and U!'

Experiences like this reinforce the importance of patience, clear communication, and humour in teaching. Children see the world through a unique lens, and as teachers, we have the privilege of guiding them as they make sense of it – one delightful question at a time.

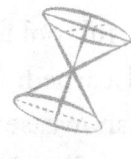

31

THE GREAT PLANET MIX-UP

Sunlight streamed through the windows of my second-year classroom, painting bright rectangles on the floor. The air practically crackled with energy – the kind that only comes when you're knee-deep in the mysteries of space. Our astronomy unit had truly ignited their young minds, even coaxing whispers of wonder from the shyest corners of the room. We'd taken our ordinary classroom and transformed it into a cosmic wonderland: a sprawling, papier-mâché solar system hung suspended from the ceiling, a vibrant mobile of painted planets swaying gently above our heads, each one a swirling masterpiece of colour and glitter. Little explorers navigated this celestial landscape, their eyes wide as saucers, eager voices overlapping with shared facts and breathless discoveries about their favourite worlds.

It was time to anchor all this excitement with our trusty KWL chart – that simple yet powerful tool for mapping what we Know, Want to Know, and have Learned. Students clustered around, buzzing with readiness to showcase their newfound planetary prowess. Facts flew thick and fast: Mercury's scorching surface, Jupiter's colossal storms, Saturn's breathtaking rings – each detail recited with earnest pride.

Then it was Bruno's turn. Usually, Bruno was a human exclamation point, his hand a blur of motion, itching to share. But today, a knot seemed to form between his brows. He paused, eyes narrowed, scanning our hanging planets as if one had staged a daring escape. 'Bruno,' I prompted softly, 'tell us what you know about the planets.'

He nodded slowly, still searching the ceiling. 'I think I forgot one… the blue one. After Saturn,' he mumbled, his voice a low rumble of concentration. I offered a lifeline: 'Can you remember which planet is the seventh from the sun?' A spark ignited in his eyes. 'Yes!' he declared, a triumphant note creeping in, 'It's the seventh planet from the sun!' The name, however, remained stubbornly out of reach.

Suddenly, a jolt of pure, unadulterated inspiration seemed to zap Bruno. His hand shot into the air with the force of a rocket launch. His face didn't just beam; it glowed with the intensity of a supernova, radiating the absolute certainty of someone who had just decoded the universe's greatest secret. My own heart did a little flip. 'Yes, Bruno?' I encouraged, leaning forward, ready for the astronomical revelation.

With a grin that could rival a solar flare, Bruno projected his answer, the words ringing out with crystal clarity across the room, loud enough, I swear, for the school office to hear: 'YOUR ANUS!' The classroom dissolved into a riot of infectious giggles. I clamped my lips together, biting the inside of my cheek, fighting a losing battle against the laughter bubbling up inside me. Even the papier-mâché planets above seemed to quiver with suppressed mirth.

Managing to keep my face mostly straight, I praised Bruno's effort. 'Excellent work, Bruno! You remembered the planet's position perfectly, and you were brave enough to share your thinking. That's exactly what learning is all about!' I said, letting a small, unavoidable smile finally escape.

Sometimes, the journey through the solar system takes an unexpected, hilarious detour – the kind that sticks with you forever and serves as a brilliant, slightly inappropriate reminder of why teaching is, without a doubt, the best job in the universe.

32

THE KOALA KID STRIKES AGAIN

Alfie was the kind of student you couldn't help but adore – a lovable rascal with a twinkle in his eye, Down syndrome, and a stubborn streak that was nothing short of legendary. If things didn't go his way, you could practically set your watch by how quickly he'd dig in his heels – sometimes quite literally.

One sunny afternoon, after a minor playground scuffle with another kid, a teacher Alfie didn't recognise tried to summon him with her best 'I-mean-business' voice. Alfie's reaction? He bolted, nimbly scaling the tallest tree like a pint-sized koala on a mission.

Even when the bell rang and the playground emptied, Alfie remained perched in the branches, surveying his leafy kingdom. The teacher, now channelling her inner drill sergeant, barked at him to come down. Alfie, unfazed, simply ignored her, looking for all the world like he'd just discovered a new home.

Having taught Alfie for a while, I knew confrontation wasn't his style. Instead, I hatched a plan. Sprinting to the canteen, I grabbed an icy pole – Alfie's weakness – and raced back to the tree. 'Look what I've got for you, Alfie!' I called, waving the frozen treat like a peace offering. Alfie's eyes lit up, and he was back on solid ground in seconds, icy pole in hand and mischief in his smile.

The next day, Alfie spotted the same teacher on duty. Sensing an opportunity (and perhaps another icy pole), he orchestrated a textbook repeat: a little chaos, a dramatic tree escape, and a triumphant grin. Sure enough, the teacher, now wise to my tactics, produced a frosty bribe and coaxed him down. Alfie may have been reprimanded, but he knew he'd struck gold.

But I was onto his game. That afternoon, as the final bell rang and the kids streamed out, I snuck over and clipped the lower branches of Alfie's favourite tree. The next day, he raced over, ready for another climb – and another icy pole – but stopped short, staring up at the now-unscalable trunk. He turned to me, hands on hips, a look of dramatic betrayal on his face. For the first time, Alfie was truly stumped.

Looking back, I thought I had finally outsmarted him, but knowing Alfie, he had probably already been scheming to out-climb both the tree and me. I just hoped he hadn't spotted the flagpole.

33

ANTHONY'S LATEST 'BODY' OF WORK

The morning's sunlight streamed through the classroom window, illuminating the swirling motes of chalk dust as I wrote the day's agenda on the board. The usual quiet hum of a classroom settling in was suddenly shattered. A clamour of startled cries erupted from the hallway, followed by an urgent scrabbling sound at the door. It burst inward, and little Maya tumbled into the room, breathless and wide-eyed. 'Mr Fav! Mr Fav!' she shrieked, pointing frantically back down the corridor.

My stomach tightened instantly. 'What's wrong, Maya?' I asked, stepping away from the board, my voice coming out tighter than I'd intended. She gasped for air between words. 'Anthony... he's found a body!'

Moments later, Anthony himself appeared in the doorway, looking drained and trembling, his characteristic impish grin completely absent. I guided him gently to a chair, knelt beside him, and tried to keep my voice calm. 'Okay, Anthony. Take a deep breath for me. Now, tell me exactly what happened.'

His voice was shaky as he recounted his walk to school. He'd taken his usual route along the creek and had spotted something snagged in the thick, thorny bushes where the water narrowed. It was a figure, he insisted, fully clothed, even wearing a beanie – a body, a dead body, caught in the undergrowth. He looked genuinely traumatised. Now, Anthony had always possessed an imagination that could put a Hollywood screenwriter to shame, and his past fabrications had ranged from alien abductions to sightings of the Loch Ness Monster at the local dam. But this… this felt different. The sheer horror etched on his face was undeniable. Despite the deep-seated scepticism born from countless previous 'adventures', the distress radiating from him made it impossible to simply dismiss his claim. This required investigation.

I quickly stepped into the principal's office, relayed the alarming news, and he, bless his remarkably unflappable soul, immediately offered to cover my class. Tearing out of the school doors, I ran towards the creek, legs pumping, the image Anthony had described flashing vividly in my mind. My thoughts raced, bracing myself for something truly grim – the chilling possibility of a life violently ended, carelessly discarded in the water. Anthony's genuine distress felt too significant to ignore, and I knew I needed to verify the situation myself before involving the authorities.

Reaching the creek bank, I scrambled down the slope, my heart pounding against my ribs. And there it was, exactly as Anthony had described – a human-like form snagged in the dense bushes where the creek narrowed. A cold wave of dread washed over me. Taking a shaky breath, I cautiously approached, the air thick with the smell of damp earth and tense anticipation. As I drew nearer, my initial horror began to dissipate, dissolving into a wave of bewildered relief. It wasn't a corpse after all. It was a surprisingly realistic mannequin, fully dressed, seemingly abandoned amongst the reeds and branches – a victim, perhaps, of a very peculiar kind of littering incident.

'Well, I'll be…' I muttered aloud, a laugh bubbling up, a mix of near-hysteria and profound relief. The adrenaline drained away, leaving me feeling utterly, delightfully ridiculous. Returning to school, I delivered the news to Anthony, the principal, and my now-anxiously-awaiting class.

Anthony looked crestfallen for a moment, then slightly embarrassed, while a ripple of giggles spread through the room. I couldn't help but join in the laughter, reflecting that while Anthony's imagination might occasionally send us on wild goose chases involving well-dressed plastic figures, it certainly never made life boring.

And who knows? Maybe one day he'd stumble upon a real story, though hopefully one a little less… stiff.

34

JURASSIC LARK: THE CASE OF THE PILFERED PENNIES

School excursions are usually a blast, a chance to escape the classroom and maybe even see some dinosaurs up close at the museum. But sometimes things go hilariously off-script. One minute you're trying to explain why *T. Rex* had such tiny arms; the next you're suddenly starring in a low-stakes crime drama. This happened during a perfectly normal trip among the fossil displays when the news hit: someone had raided a donation box. And the prime suspects? Three boys who, moments before, were probably arguing about who was the coolest dinosaur.

The story that emerged was less like a professional heist and more like a clumsy caper. Apparently, two of them created a distraction – I'm picturing a sudden, dramatic collapse near a *Triceratops* skeleton – while the third, the alleged mastermind, got busy. His weapon of choice? A tiny screwdriver attachment from a Swiss Army knife, because apparently, ten-year-olds are surprisingly resourceful when it comes to minor larceny. With this miniature tool, he'd reportedly popped open the back of the box and snagged some cash.

Gathering the trio, I expected a quick confession. Instead, their faces went completely blank, as if someone had hit the 'off' switch on their expressions. A thick, awkward silence descended, heavy with unspoken guilt and the faint smell of the dinosaur exhibit. Clearly, questioning them as a group wasn't going to work. It was time for the classic manoeuvre: separate and interrogate.

I took the first boy aside, putting on my best 'concerned but cool' face. 'So,' I began gently, 'about that money box…' His eyes immediately darted anywhere but at me. 'Wasn't me!' he mumbled, fixing his gaze on a particularly dusty pterodactyl model. I leaned in secretively. 'Hmm,' I mused, 'that's odd, because your buddies seemed pretty sure it was you.' The impact was immediate. His face lit up with panic. 'NO! It was John! He used his knife thingy!' Betrayal, swift and brutal, had landed.

Next up was suspect number two. I asked him the same question, receiving the same instant denial, though maybe a little more practised this time. 'Nope, wasn't me,' he chirped, already fidgeting. I hit him with the same line: 'Funny, because the others linked you to it.' He blinked, feigning shock with Oscar-worthy skill. 'JOHN!' he declared. 'It was definitely John! With his little knife!' The story was solidifying, built on the rapidly dissolving foundation of ten-year-old friendship.

Finally, it was John's turn. He swaggered over, trying to look bored. 'Money? What money?' he scoffed, attempting a nonchalant shrug that looked more like a nervous twitch. He was doing okay until I dropped the bomb. 'John,' I said calmly, 'your two friends? They both said it was you.' The swagger evaporated instantly. His shoulders slumped. And then, like a punchline delivered by fate, a tiny glint of metal peeked out of his pocket. The Swiss Army knife. There it was. The tool, the evidence, the nail in the coffin. Game over.

Looking back, it was a miniature drama played out among prehistoric giants – a quick lesson in how quickly childhood alliances crumble under pressure and how terrible ten-year-olds are at lying. The actual theft was minor, but the quick finger-pointing and the comically obvious evidence revealed in John's pocket were a funny, if slightly exasperating, reminder that even a trip to see dinosaurs can include unexpected life lessons in basic detective work.

35

JUST ANOTHER DAY IN DOB CITY: THE HEARING SCARE

Yard duty: the glamorous, high-stakes world of patrolling the concrete jungle. My assigned territory was the junior playground, a place staff affectionately – or perhaps battle-wearily – nicknamed 'Dob City'. True to its reputation, it was a daily tide of tiny humans filing reports: 'He looked at me funny!', 'She hogged the swing!', 'He... breathed on my sandcastle!' But this particular afternoon brought a crisis of genuinely alarming proportions.

A small figure, maybe Prep-aged, stumbled towards me, their face a crumpled roadmap of pure, utter despair, tears flowing like tiny, unstoppable tributaries. 'Oh dear,' I thought, bracing myself for another gripping tale from the Dob City Gazette. 'Here we go.'

I knelt down, trying to seem as gentle as possible. 'Hey there, little one. What's all this? What's the matter?'

Through hiccupping sobs and dramatic gasps, she wailed, 'I've... hiccup... lost... sob... my hearing!'

My internal alarm bells didn't just ring, they performed a full-blown mariachi band concert. Her hearing?! On my watch?! This wasn't a minor playground infraction; this was a potential medical emergency! Trying desperately to keep the panic out of my voice, I asked, 'Your hearing? Oh, goodness gracious. Can you hear me right now?'

'Yes!' she replied, the tears still streaming, which seemed... well, counter-intuitive.

'Well, then,' I said, a tidal wave of relief washing over me, nearly knocking me off my crouch. 'See? There's absolutely nothing wrong with your hearing at all. You can hear me perfectly.'

'But I lost them!' she insisted, spinning dramatically and pointing a trembling finger towards a vast, treacherous desert known as the sandpit. 'If I don't find them, Mummy will be very, very cross!'

Lost... them? Them? Not her hearing, but them? What them? My brain, just recovering from the 'lost hearing' scare, now grappled with this new auditory mystery. 'Lost... them?' I clarified, a flicker of something resembling understanding beginning to dawn. 'You mean... something you wear? Like... earrings?'

'YES!' she declared, a sudden, sharp note of pure exasperation cutting clean through her tears.

And just like that, the great 'hearing' crisis of Dob City, the potential medical emergency, the source of such profound despair, boiled down to a simple case of missing jewellery. Just another day navigating the complex, pun-laden world on the front lines of primary school, where communication is indeed key, and sometimes, you just need to listen very, very carefully… especially for the punchline.

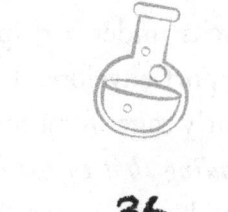

36

THE FINE, WET LINE BETWEEN GOOD AND BAD

Mid-year report time always brought a certain, palpable tension. It was the period defined by the impending delivery of official judgment. Back then, before the sterile efficiency of laser printers and digital PDFs, reports arrived as glorious, messy carbon copies. They were smudgy, faint, and utterly unique – each one a slightly blurred snapshot of a student's academic standing. The routine was predictable: reports were distributed with solemn instructions that the children were to take them home for careful parental review, followed a few days later by the 'Spanish Inquisition' of parent–teacher interviews.

On one particular afternoon, the heavens opened just as the final bell rang. Students streamed out in a chaotic, rain-dodging exodus. I watched from my classroom window as the downpour intensified. And then I saw Simon.

He hadn't gone far. Just outside the shelter of the doorway, huddled near the bike racks under a dripping awning, he was wrestling with his large report envelope. I could see him tearing it open, head bent low, clearly eager for a sneak peek before facing the parental gaze. *He's reading that in the rain!* By the time that report reached his parents' hands, it would be a soggy, illegible mess. The ink would bleed, the carbon copies blurring into a grey smudge. A disaster in triplicate.

The next day, the rain had passed, but the air still hummed with anticipation. I addressed the class, asking about the reception of the reports and if there were any burning questions before the gauntlet of interviews. Simon's hand shot up, tentative but urgent. 'Mr Fav,' he began, his voice slightly hesitant. 'My Dad… he was a bit unsure about a word in my report.'

Ah, here we go, I thought, a weary sense of inevitability washing over me. The smudge. I remembered seeing him hunched over that report in the rain. 'He couldn't quite read it,' Simon continued, confirming my suspicion. 'It was a bit… smudged.'

'Okay,' I said, trying to sound helpful rather than smugly predictive. 'What's the word?' Simon paused, a flicker of genuine confusion on his face. 'Well,' he said, looking down at his desk, 'he's not sure whether the report says I'm… diligent… or delinquent.'

There was a moment of silence followed by a ripple of suppressed giggles from the class. I blinked, processing this rather significant ambiguity. Diligent: hardworking, conscientious, a model student. Delinquent: troublesome, law-breaking, a potential future problem. Quite a difference. It struck me then how much meaning could hinge on a single, smudged word, especially when rendered illegible by something as simple as a sudden downpour and a student's impatience. It was a funny reminder that communication, even via official reports, isn't always clear-cut, and sometimes the biggest misunderstandings stem from the smallest, wettest details. And perhaps, just perhaps, it perfectly highlighted the fine line some students seem to walk between those two very different descriptors.

37

JULIA'S FEATHERED FIESTA

During show and tell, little Julia, eyes wide with excitement, transported us all to Spain with tales of a dazzling performance she'd attended with her parents. As a teacher, it was wonderful to see how completely absorbed she was in the memory, painting a vivid picture of Spanish musicians coaxing passionate rhythms from their guitars and dancers bursting onto the stage in a whirlwind of swirling skirts and rhythmic stomping. The sheer energy and vibrant colours of the show were utterly captivating, leaving everyone in the room spellbound. Julia was particularly mesmerised by the electrifying dancing, explaining how it was such a powerful part of their culture.

Intrigued by her description, and keen to encourage her specific recall, I asked if she knew the style of dance they performed. Julia took a deep breath, a look of absolute certainty on her face, and declared with unwavering confidence, 'Oh yes! It's called... flamingo dancing!' I smiled inwardly; her conviction was utterly charming, even if the name wasn't quite right. It was a perfect example of how children confidently piece together new information, sometimes with delightful, colourful results, and a reminder of the vibrant, slightly misunderstood world they inhabit.

38

THE DAY THE KIDS DELIVERED THE F-BOMB

Living in the school neighbourhood inevitably blurs the lines between work and home. Often, this merging is quite pleasant – a friendly wave from a student cycling past, or a quick question about long division even as I wrestle the bins to the curb. It's generally a welcome feeling, a constant, gentle hum of being part of the community.

While weekdays often follow a predictable rhythm, Saturdays possess a different, often chaotic, energy. Take a recent Saturday, for instance. I was happily immersed in the simple bliss of being home, deep in a peaceful domestic task, my mind blessedly free from complex thoughts. Then, suddenly, bang bang BANG on the front door. This wasn't a polite knock; it was urgent, frantic. Interrupted mid-task, I yanked the door open, bracing myself for whatever emergency awaited.

Standing there were three small, grubby faces from my Year 4 class, looking remarkably like they'd just survived a minor skirmish. 'Right then,' I said, attempting to project calm while my brain processed the sudden, violent assault on my door. 'Is everything all right? What's going on?'

Before I could even register their indignant, puff-cheeked expressions, one piped up, his voice cracking with pure outrage: 'Mr Fav! There was this BIG boy down the road and he told us to tell you that you can… you can GET EFFED!'

I froze. A nine-year-old on my porch had just delivered an adult swear word with furious conviction. My brain, only moments before focused on laundry, short-circuited with shock. 'Okay,' I finally managed, my voice feeling utterly alien. 'Did… this "big boy"… know who I am?'

Three heads shook vigorously. 'No way! He was just being mean!'

'Right,' I mumbled, wrestling with this bizarre neighbourhood development. 'Because that's a remarkably aggressive message for a stranger to send.' Then, the quietest student added the crucial, clarifying footnote. 'We argued with him because he was being mean, and he swore at me, so we said we were going to tell you!'

'Ah,' I said, the penny dropping with a loud clang of pure awkwardness. They hadn't simply run an errand; they'd used me as a human shield, a counter-threat in their playground dispute. Awkwardness escalated from mild discomfort to a desperate wish for the porch to swallow me whole.

But despite my internal monologue screaming about my ruined quiet Saturday and the sudden expansion of my duties into foul-mouthed neighbourhood negotiations, I had to be the grown-up. 'Look, boys,' I said, stepping carefully. 'I appreciate you sticking up for each other. And I even admire the audacious creativity of using your teacher as leverage.'

I continued, trying to navigate this unexpected minefield. 'But this problem? The one with the mean boy and the swearing? It doesn't actually involve me. An older boy was mean and swore? That's not fair, but the best people to tell are your parents. They know how to handle things like that. Let's keep Mr Fav and his quiet Saturday out of these… complex negotiations, okay?'

Their faces fell, the glorious vision of Mr Fav descending as a righteous angel of vengeance clearly evaporating. They mumbled thanks that sounded suspiciously like disappointment, shuffled off the porch, and headed back down the road, leaving me alone once more.

As I closed the door, I leaned against it, taking a deep breath. I'd thought my biggest professional challenge was teaching fractions. Instead, I discovered my reputation extended well beyond the school gates, making me the unexpected target of an 'effing' delivered by a child I hadn't known existed ten minutes earlier. Some Saturdays, you just can't win against the spectacularly unexpected.

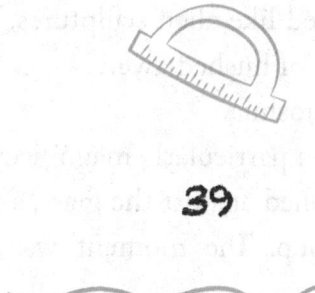

39

AQUARIUM AWKWARDNESS: THE JOSHUA EFFECT

The air in the classroom practically vibrated with pure, unadulterated excitement, a potent mix of sugar-fuelled anticipation and the sheer thrill of escaping multiplication tables. Aquarium day! We finally boarded the bus, a noisy metal beast that rumbled and groaned its way through the snarled, honking arteries of city traffic. The journey itself was an adventure, a symphony of off-key singing and shouts of 'Are we there yet?!' every thirty seconds.

Finally, we spilled out onto the footpath, buzzing with energy, and entered the cool, dim, magical world of the aquarium. We split into our carefully orchestrated small groups, each clutching the hand of a bewildered parent volunteer, and plunged into the watery labyrinth. Giant windows transported us into another dimension, filled with amazingly vibrant fish darting among swaying kelp forests, ancient-looking sea turtles gliding past, and coral colonies that looked like alien sculptures. It was genuinely breathtaking, a moment of hushed awe...

And then, there was Joshua.

As we paused before a particularly magnificent, large octopus, its powerful arms suctioned against the glass, a profound silence fell over our little group. The moment was perfect. Serene. Educational.

Joshua, bless his innocent soul, chose this precise instant to unleash his observation upon the world.

'WHOA!' he boomed, his voice echoing through the quiet recesses of the aquarium, startling nearby visitors. 'LOOK at the size of the TESTICLES on that octopus!'

Silence. A shudder of stunned, horrified silence. Every single second-grader's head whipped around, eyes wide with a mix of confusion and burgeoning fascination. Parents froze, their smiles melting into expressions ranging from panicked embarrassment to barely stifled laughter. Other aquarium patrons, drawn by the sudden shout, now peered with intense curiosity at the octopus... and then back at our mortified group leader (me).

My internal panic siren shrieked. My face felt like it was on fire. I leaned down quickly, attempting to maintain an air of calm professionalism while simultaneously wanting to vanish into a puff of smoke. 'Joshua,' I whispered urgently, trying to steer him towards the correct terminology without causing further international incident. 'Matey, those are called tentacles. He has eight strong tentacles.'

Joshua blinked up at me, utterly unfazed by the collective gasp or the sudden crowd gathering around us. He glanced back at the octopus, then shrugged matter-of-factly. 'Yeah,' he conceded, nodding. 'But they're still pretty big!'

Teaching second grade is a daily tightrope walk between structured learning and the unpredictable chaos of tiny, unfiltered humans. You plan, you prepare, you envision smooth, educational experiences. And then a child loudly identifies an octopus's appendages as something you'd only expect to hear mumbled by a teenager. In a public place. In front of dozens of strangers. You spend years mastering classroom management, only to realise that the most challenging moments often happen outside those four walls. You learn to stifle your own laughter while correcting wildly inappropriate vocabulary, to manage the reactions of parents and strangers, and to somehow pivot back to the wonders of marine biology as if nothing just happened. It's exhausting, it's hilarious, and honestly, it's why I'll never forget that particular field trip. Or Joshua. Or that highly… *endowed*… octopus.

EPILOGUE

And so, with the final page turned on *Chalk Full of Laughs*, I find myself looking back on a career that felt, at times, less like a profession and more like a high-wire act performed daily amidst a shower of chalk dust and unexpected life lessons.

Wading through the vast, unruly archive of my mind for these stories has been, shall we say, an adventure.

Those classroom capers – the laugh-out-loud moments right alongside the quiet, heartfelt connections – are etched forever in my memory. They'll always remind me of the truly special, often utterly chaotic, ride that was teaching.

I sincerely hope you had as much fun reading these tales as I had digging them out… just promise you won't ask me to grade your enjoyment.

ABOUT THE AUTHOR

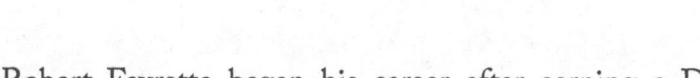

Robert Favretto began his career after earning a Diploma of Teaching (Primary) from the State College of Victoria in Coburg in 1980, later enhancing his credentials with a Bachelor of Education from the Phillip Institute of Technology in 1987.

For decades, Robert taught across all year levels throughout Victoria, including a valuable period in special education that honed his patience and creativity. Beyond teaching roles like PE specialist and assistant principal, his varied work history includes stints as a petrol station attendant, strawberry picker, Kodak production line operator, and manager of a Movieland video store. This diverse background demonstrates his wide-ranging skills, from selecting a good film to finding the ripest berry.

A lifelong sports enthusiast, Robert has participated in a wide range of activities, including squash, spear fishing, marathon running, indoor cricket, mixed netball, and stair climbing.

Having navigated countless flights of stairs over the years, he now appreciates the convenience of a lift – a testament to the wisdom that often accompanies age (and sore knees).

In 1998, driven by a desire to transform his wealth of classroom experiences into published stories, Robert earned a professional writing for children qualification. While he stepped away from full-time teaching in 2017, he remains connected to the education world as a relief teacher, ensuring his narratives stay fresh and current. When he's not busy writing, Robert delights audiences at schools, libraries, and festivals with his trademark lively and engaging talks and presentations.

www.ingramcontent.com/pod-product-compliance
Lightning Source LLC
Chambersburg PA
CBHW011300070526
44584CB00027BA/3793